I0684444

# Soaring

## an ANTHOLOGY

Published by the Antelope Valley Writers Association
Palmdale, CA 93551

Please visit our website: http://avwritersassociation.wordpress.com

Front cover artwork, *Up and Beyond* © Carole Rosefelt
Front cover design by Doreen Kennedy

Library of Congress Control Number:  2013957476

ISBN:  978-0-615-93759-5

# DEDICATION

This book is dedicated to our home, the Antelope Valley, and to the hard-working men and women of the aviation and aerospace industries which helped the cities of Lancaster and Palmdale to soar. From breaking the sound barrier, to space shuttles and stealth aircraft, the Antelope Valley is the site of many major aeronautical accomplishments.

This book is also dedicated to the Lancaster Library, a branch of the County of Los Angeles Library System, for providing a meeting place for the Antelope Valley Writers Association, and to libraries everywhere for providing a portal to knowledge. May they forever enrich our lives.

## About the ANTELOPE VALLEY WRITERS ASSOCIATION

Every Wednesday afternoon a diverse group of people and personalities fill a meeting room at the Lancaster Public Library. They are doctors and teachers, homemakers and painters, cooks and firefighters, librarians and salespersons – all with a gift for storytelling. Three common threads bind them: a love of life in the high desert of Southern California, a desire to share their writings, and the camaraderie that evolves from sharing hopes, fears, hearts, and dreams. This is the Antelope Valley Writers Association (AVWA) where words are meant to be shared.

Visit our website: http://www.avwritersassociation.wordpress.com

# ACKNOWLEDGMENTS

The AVWA would like to thank the following people whose hard work and dedication made this anthology a reality:

- Patricia Alexander for her input and guidance on this project, for chairing our weekly meetings, and for being the ideal hostess – always there with a smile.

- Doreen Kennedy, the anthology project manager, for taking on the collecting, editing, formatting, and publishing tasks.

- Oleg Kagan, the founder of the Antelope Valley Writers Group (now the Antelope Valley Writers Association), for his expert advice and editing.

- Carole Rosefelt for allowing us to use her original artwork on the cover. Her painting invites us all to reach new heights, thus the title and theme of this anthology – *Soaring*.

About the cover artist:

Carole Rosefelt studied at Layton Art School and Cardinal Stritch College. Her art career as an award-winning painter has spanned more than 40 years. A native of Milwaukee, WI, she now resides in Florida, and is active in the local art community in the Tampa Bay area. Carole is a member of Tampa Bay Surface Design Guild, PAVA, and Studio 1212. She continues to inspire artists as an instructor at the Dunedin Fine Art Center.

# CONTENTS

# MARY DENNING

Mary Denning, a ten year resident of the Antelope Valley, is a native of Southern California where she and husband, Joe, raised their six children. She is a graduate of California State University Northridge with a degree in Art. Her artwork has been exhibited and sold at galleries in Cambria, Santa Cruz, and the San Fernando Mission, where she currently she has a painting on display as part of their art collection.

After retiring from her job with the Los Angeles Library System, she decided to try her hand at writing. Her first attempt won her recognition in a local newspaper. She now enjoys writing short stories and poetry, and was recently recognized by the City of Palmdale for winning their inaugural "Walk On Words" poetry contest. Mary's winning poem, *What Beauty Holds Us Captive Here*, is preserved in cement in the city square and is featured on the following page.

## WHAT BEAUTY HOLDS US CAPTIVE HERE

What beauty holds us captive here?

Might the ancient antelope know?

Or seek ye out the smart Black Crows

Windy echoes from long ago

From ghostly herds of deer that flow

But stopped to graze and disappear

Kitanemuk of old revere

Snowcapped mountains that were so near

And Joshua trees and cacti rare

And fields of wild colors there

Where golden poppies fare

And mix with Blue Lupine to pair

They said a rainbow led us here.

## GRANMA'S BAG OF TRICKS

When Granma's called to babysit
She just brings out her bag of tricks
If called upon to referee
'Cause little tykes will disagree
And nothing seems to stop a row
She hollers out "don't have a cow"
Success may not appear right now
"Regroup!" she goes and yells it loud
"Mustard and Pickles, Mustard and Pickles"
Surprised they stop, their laughter ripples
Come on she says let's have popsicles
And when it's time for them to go
They pout and cry it can't be so
So Granma finds a toy to go
And peace and harmony bestows
On little ones that parents know
Once in the car will settle so
If those that hang behind are slow
Refusing yet to get along and go
Granma yells this challenge so
"Last one out is a rotten egg"
That wraps it up as she waves hooray!

## JAMES OUR ONE MAN BAND

Play this please they beg and tease

Challenge accepted for James it's a breeze

Youth is no handicap nor can autism hold back

Performance excels with piano fortes

Brain to the fingers cooperate please

Both hands play with remarkable ease

His gifts are displayed with intention to please

Neither notes to be read nor lessons to be had

He performs to the accolades that are at hand

Dexterity, creativity pour forth from this lad

And sweet notes escalade from a Slide Trombone

And from Trumpets, Bassoons and Harmonicas he knows

Encouragement follows with fast clapping hands

Because James, we love, is our One Man Band

## THE GREEN, GREEN HILLS OF YORE

Across the Seas and far away
A visit we did take
Seeking family dare we say?
More for our loved ones' sake
In the land of Sacred places
And ancient Hunter Bands

But finding friends we made new plans
'Cause friends we love to make
With welcome greets and helping hands
We toured the country lakes
In the land of Sacred places
And ancient Hunter Bands

Found burial sites of ancient kings
At mounds and burial rings
Where Ulsters died and fought for things
That peace and glory bring
In the land of Sacred places
And ancient Hunter Bands

St. Patrick into Ireland came
Revered and loved he stayed
The shamrock used became his fame
To Trinity he prayed
In the land of Sacred places
And ancient Hunter Bands

Two churches stand on opposite hills
Both honoring Patrick there
Not of one faith, but in good will
For Armagh's ancient care
In the land of Sacred places
And ancient Hunter Bands

County Armagh lay before us
Ancient seat of kings
Sons of Fergus, mighty warriors
Celtic rituals did bring
In the land of Sacred places
And ancient Hunter Bands

And tales told of battles fought
Where Celtics died for lands
And Brian Boru their leader sought
Victory for his Clans
In the land of Sacred places
And ancient Hunter Bands

Where music sung told tales of old
Sad songs about yon wars
And dear loves lost laid in the cold
Tears shed across the shores
In the land of Sacred places
And ancient Hunter Bands

And whiskey drank and often sold
For solace hoped to find
Yet in this land of green, green hills
Our hearts remain entwined
Forever held in memories
Of families good and kind
Connected kin from long ago
These Irish hearts will pine
In the land of Sacred places
And ancient Hunter Bands


And up above the dark green cross
We watched the raven soar
Above the peat and wet green moss
Reminders of folklore
In the land of Sacred places
And ancient Hunter Bands


Of tales we've heard of many wars
From the green, green hills of yore.

## CLOUDS

When do clouds come out to play?
I'd like to think it's every day
Do they see me when I see them?
Would they wish to meet and say:
How's the air around your way?
As I would seek to lie within
The softness of their Cumulus
Perhaps the high Cirrus Clouds
Have found a way to slow them down
From Jet Streams pushing round and round
Moving clouds a way too fast
So very far below I cry, stop I want to see
Please wait for me
I only want to climb aboard and flee
To distant lands across the sea
Where Stratospheres above the clouds
Look down and sadly wonder why they alone
Are too cold to form some friendship clouds
But I could wave as I ride by
To let them know I sympathize
When skies look down and I look up
Our smiles could warm the skies so much
This friendship bond unites us such
For clouds and me to keep in touch.
And evermore a friendship born.

# STEVE ORDWAY

Steve Ordway's honorable career as a fireman with the Los Angeles City Fire Department spanned twenty-five years, twelve of which were spent as a paramedic on an ambulance. He had the distinction of being one of the first paramedic firefighters and, due to a shortage of civilian paramedics, was detailed to work on a rescue ambulance for most of his assigned shifts.

His many experiences responding to emergency calls in south central Los Angeles and Hollywood have provided material for hundreds of tales, some grisly and some hilarious. Steve's wife encouraged him to write about these incidents, which he is compiling into a book on the day-to-day life of a Los Angeles fireman.

FELINE MISSLE

The black column of smoke made the location easy to find that summer afternoon. It was my first day as acting captain at Engine 93. I was lucky to have veteran firemen in Tom, Brian, and Joe on the crew.

During the fuel shortage of the 1970s, a contractor had stored gasoline in 55 gallon drums in a carport next to his single family dwelling in Tarzana, California. His teenage son pumped a few gallons into an open bucket. His Harley was next to the house. As he toted the fuel the ten feet from barrel to bike, he passed the water heater that was also located there.

Gasoline fumes are present when the temperature is above minus 69 degrees Fahrenheit, which it always is in the Valley. These fumes are heavier than air and will leave a vapor trail on a windless day, such as that day. When the water heater ignited the fumes, the boy discovered that he was standing astride the vapor trail. The flash caused him to panic; he dropped the bucket, spilled its contents, and turned the carport into a sea of flames. He fled the area with his pants on fire.

Rolling up to the location, we passed a boy on a bicycle. As we stopped at the hydrant the excited lad rode up to the tailboard, unseen by Brian, the large sized crewman who was to lay the line. The burly fireman stepped off with the heavy four way valve and a fold of hose, directly onto the bike. We could hear his cursing over the sound of the motor as Brian, the hose, the boy and the bicycle ended up in a tangled heap on the asphalt. We drove the engine to the fire with its hose stringing out behind it.

The flames had broken a side window and were entering the house. Tom took a hose line to the front door. As soon as it was charged, I kicked the locked door open, and we rushed in to save the structure.

I had once heard the word "synchronicity," and on that day, I experienced it in action. The line loaded. I kicked the door. From the carport, a gasoline barrel exploded with a loud boom. A cat flew out the front door.

It was three feet off the ground and going 80 miles per hour. It continued out of sight. If it had hit either Tom or I, we would have surely been injured. I would hate to be the one to have to make out that medical report.

Recovering from the shock of the rocketing cat, Tom and I entered the hallway leading to the fully involved room. The smoke vented out through the front door rather quickly, and we could see flames licking out of the burning room and flowing overhead, above us, hugging the ceiling. Seeing this common place phenomenon in structure fires always made me uneasy.

We advanced the loaded inch and a half line down the hallway. The heat drove us to our knees. At the doorway we set the nozzle on a spray pattern, opened it up and swished the water upward into the inferno. Knowing that one gallon of water makes 1600 gallons of steam, we were confident that the fire would be quickly smothered. All we had to do was stay clear of the doorway, or we would be steamed.

"Bang, bang, bang!" Explosions resounded from the room. It sounded like a war had broken out. "Bang, bang, bang!" The detonations continued accompanied by fast flying objects. The resident's guns and ammunition were stored in that room, and the exploding shells and flying bullets turned our fire into a battlefield. No wonder the cat left in such a hurry. He must have known about the ammo dump.

Cleaning up after the fireworks ended and the area had cooled down, we discovered that the owner possessed a formidable arsenal of weapons. Later, all of the guns were checked out as legal to own.

I noticed a pair of jeans, still smoldering, laying on the front lawn. Rescue 100 had already transported the owner's son for treatment of some minor, albeit strategically located burns.

Fortunately, the only injuries incurred to any firemen at that incident were Brian's bruised elbows when he fell over the kid's bike. I think he probably ended any desire that boy might have had of becoming a firefighter.

The cat had not returned by the time we left.

## EDITH

The sedan slammed into the back of her van sending it into oncoming traffic. A cement truck plowed into the front, pushing her vehicle backward for one hundred feet, according to the skid marks. As the cab of the van crushed inward, the dashboard collapsed onto her lap, pinning her in the seat. The driver's side door was forced open by the impact and the four-foot wide opening was reduced to less than twelve inches.

I could see her gray hair through the cloud of steam that was coming from the ruptured radiator. She was middle-aged, wearing a salmon colored waitress's uniform with "Edith" etched into her nameplate. Her head rolled from side to side. She was mercifully semiconscious. I smelled that sickening odor that I have often encountered at bloody incidents.

Andy threw off his turnout coat and helmet, and then dived head first into the cab from the passenger's side. He wriggled under the dash, sliding in her blood. He yelled out that he could see the bare bones of her knees sticking up above her thighs. My stomach churned at the shock of how bad this situation was. I had no idea of how to get her out of that vehicle.

"Call for the Heavy U," shouted the captain.

The Heavy Utility is a rig with specialized extrication equipment. We had just learned, last week, that we were among the first to get the "Jaws of Life" tool. Now we needed it. We had to wait while it responded from ten miles away. Even with red lights and siren, we knew the rush hour traffic would make this wait an eternity.

The stress was apparent on the faces of the firemen as we administered oxygen and took her vitals. Although her eyes were open, she couldn't respond to me. She groaned loudly and continued moving her head from side to side in unimaginable agony.

"They'd better get here soon," whispered Joe, the engineer, "or we're going to lose her."

Fortunately, the steering column had shortened due to the 'crush design' that had been built into it as a safety measure, but it would still have to be dealt with. She could breathe okay, but the steering wheel was pressed against her chest and was hampering our efforts.

We wrapped her up in a blanket to protect her from the shards as we removed what was left of the window glass. We had the gurney, backboard and bandages all set up for when the Heavy U finally arrived. We feared she would bleed out once the clamping action of the steel dashboard was released from her legs.

The police had closed off the street. The cars that had been inching by with their rubbernecking occupants, their faces plastered against their windows, had been rerouted. It was a surrealistic scene. We were surrounded by the din of the emergency. The throbbing of the fire truck engines, the staccato blinking of the emergency lights, the periodic messages blaring from the rig's radios all added to the tension. We were completely helpless awaiting the Jaws, and our patient desperately needed medical attention.

Andy, with the shoulder of his uniform soaked with blood, had just managed to unbolt the driver's door from the Dodge when the radio crackled with, "Heavy U 88 on scene."

I was relieved to see Leroy hurrying up, lugging a big steel tool. It was tethered by its hydraulic hoses to a pump being carried by Dave. These two men were the dream team in rescue work. Their mechanical ability was renowned. They operated D-9 Caterpillars during brush fires as part of their duties. They handled the Jaws with the skill and confidence of many hours of training. As Dave tended the gasoline driven hydraulic pump, the size of an electrical generator, Leroy put the jaws in the squeezed down doorway.

"Will you need wooden blocks for bracing?" I asked.

"Stand back, this baby doesn't need any help," he said.

The fluid pumping through the high pressure hose expanded those jaws, miraculously unfolding that cab, raising the dash and the steering wheel at an amazing rate. It was the first time that I had seen this impressive tool in action, and I believe it was its first use at an emergency in this area. We slid our patient out gently, fearing what we would find as her legs were revealed.

Her bleeding turned out to be minimal. Either clotting had occurred, or she was running dry of fluids. Her weak, rapid pulse indicated the latter. Carefully and quickly we encased her mangled legs in cardboard splints, straightened the limbs and packed the exposed bones with saturated pads.

After we got a large bore I.V. established, we raced to the nearby hospital with siren blaring and lights flashing. Her condition remained unchanged during transport. I squeezed the bag of saline going into her vein, trying to replace the blood loss more quickly.

Having radioed ahead, the staff was ready to receive Edith when we arrived at the hospital. She was whisked away out of sight. I'm sure she went straight to the operating room. I found out later that she survived this ghastly ordeal, but I don't know how her leg injuries turned out, as she was transferred to UCLA Medical Center. I wonder if she lost them, or if she was wheelchair bound for life.

It has always bothered me, not knowing.

## JIM'S WILD RIDE

Jim Baylis was a tillerman. He drove the back wheels of the aerial ladder truck. He was also responsible for the maintenance of the apparatus, the tools and equipment, and even the wooden ladders. He also had explicit firefighting duties at emergencies.

Jim was one of the best and most conscientious men at the station. His nickname was "Rip," after Rip Van Winkle. This was because he was known for his ability, after finishing all of his chores, to be able to sit down and immediately fall asleep. Some speculated that he suffered from narcolepsy, but the truth was that he worked an extra job every day off in order to make ends meet. Those long, exhausting hours gave him the ability to conk out at any opportunity.

I developed that ability myself after becoming a paramedic and experiencing sleep deprivation. Jim's sleeping led to the other trait that he was known for, snoring. In the big, long dormitory that had beds for twelve men, Jim was on one end and the rest of us as far away as possible.

A Mel Gibson movie, titled *Thunderdome*, was popular at this time. It featured an enclosure into which two combatants would engage in mortal combat. The crowd would chant, "Two men enter, one man leaves." Some wag posted a sign on the dormitory door, proclaiming:

## THUNDERDORM
### Twelve men enter, eleven men leave.

For reasons unknown to me, the administration had provided Fire Station 93 with the oldest truck in the department, a 1953 Peter Persch. We got along with it pretty well, but it went in for repair one day. The radiator had developed a leak so bad that the autofireman who drove it placed a bucket underneath to catch the water. He then tied a piece of rope from the bucket's handle to the rig's steering wheel, that way no one would forget to pour the water back into the radiator, or drive over the bucket.

When it went in for repair, we got an even older relic in its place. The only leak that this one had was from the air tank that operated the brakes. Knowing this, the driver would always run the engine to build up air pressure before moving.

One day, we got a dispatch for a house fire on nearby Chalk Hill. The antique truck was leading the task force. As it turned onto the steep grade leading to the address, some excited children were on the sidewalk. They jumped up and down at the sound of the siren, and as the old rig passed them, they took off running up the hill, beating our museum piece to the fire!

The house was well involved. It was a working fire that, after the knock down, would occupy us with overhaul for hours. During this time, the ladder truck was parked on a grade, in gear, with chock blocks behind the wheels.

With the overhaul completed, and all the tools back on the rig, Jim climbed into the tiller bucket. The driver raised his hand, signaling for the starter button to be pushed. As a safety measure in ladder trucks, both driver and tiller man must simultaneously engage the starter. Unfortunately, while boarding the rig, the firemen picked up the chock blocks.

The driver put the transmission in neutral, and as he raised his hand the truck began slowly rolling backwards down the hill. The air had bled off, and they had no brakes. The driver tried to jam the transmission back in gear without success. As the truck gained speed, Jim tried to navigate the steep, winding road with cars parked on both sides. Seeing what was happening, I gave chase down the hill on foot. Jim was my best friend, and this didn't look good!

Although in a panic mode that escalated with the speed of the now runaway truck, this exemplary tiller man deftly negotiated the curves while traveling backwards. Seeing that they were about to encounter cars coming up the hill, Jim made a split second decision to leave the road, hop the curb, and arrest their motion by steering into a bushy tree. He, along with the rear thirty feet of the rig, disappeared into the branches.

Leaping onto the turntable, I clawed my way down the ladder, blinded by the foliage. Nearing the tiller bucket, I was greatly relieved to hear, "Oh, sugar," the strongest expletive that ever leaves Jim's lips. I then knew that my buddy was alright. No firemen, nor civilians, required medical assistance. I believe that the city buried the truck.

# PAT ALEXANDER

Born and raised in Buffalo, New York, and having lived in several U.S. states and in Europe, Pat Alexander is happy to call the Antelope Valley's high desert her home.

Pat is multi-talented; she is an artist as well as a published author, and also worked in the entertainment industry. While living abroad she studied art in Milan, Paris, and Dubrovnik, and has exhibited and sold her paintings worldwide. She was also a principal entertainer, singing and dancing for eight years with the Folies Bergère and other stage shows in Las Vegas.

She discovered her writing talent in California, where she began composing short stories and poetry. Pat recently published her first book, *Pollywogs and Green Things Growing*. As with her artwork, she finds inspiration for writing in raw nature, animals, and in observing humankind. She is also inspired by her two beautiful daughters, Kathleen and Adriana, and granddaughter Gabrielle.

## THE IRISH TENOR

Grandpa had a large pink and white cameo ring in a gold filigree setting that he wore on Sundays and on other special occasions. I enjoyed looking at it as I sat on his lap. He allowed me to comb and brush his gray, thinning hair and didn't mind my ministrations as I worked diligently to slick it back just so.

Grandpa was a good-natured fellow and usually had a few corny jokes for me or he would sing songs. "What would you like to hear Patty", he would ask. "How about, "When Irish eyes are smiling"? Or "Peggy O'Neil"?

"I don't care Grandpa," I said. "I love all of your songs."

He would stand up and pretend that he was on a stage. "Now make sure you point the lampshade in my direction," he told me. I knew that this was my cue to aim the floor lamp towards Grandpa so he could deliver his song in a spotlight like he used to do when he was a professional Irish tenor. The light caught a glimmer of the gold tooth he had in the front of his mouth. His blue eyes twinkled as he belted out a rousing rendition of "Sweet Rosie O'Grady."

Grandma came into the living room to listen awhile. She used to accompany Grandpa when he sang at church halls and venues. They were a popular twosome and very talented. The only problem was that Grandma was jealous of the women that swooned over her husband when he sang. She was very possessive of him.

Grandpa said, "Come here Florence, and help me out, would you please? Our granddaughter is waiting to hear the old songs."

She melted when he spoke to her in his special soft voice. Florence had married Albert for his Irish good looks and she meant to keep him hers forever. Sometimes you could hear them argue in their bedroom at night.

"Al, why did you pay attention to that Bessie Corrigan at the party?"

He would protest, "But I didn't Florence. It's not my fault that she likes my singing, is it?" He would give her a kiss and tell her, "You are my only girl, you know that, don't you?" She would be happy then and quiet down for the night.

## CRYSTAL BEACH

The monkey lady on the hill is a little bit crazy
    Her antique record player she is winding, winding.
The song she plays is drifting out the window nineteen twenties style.
    We hear the melody as we pass by on the way to
        Crystal Beach.


The Crystal Beach boat, it floats from Buffalo, it floats to Canada.
    Back and forth it goes.
At the gate you buy your ticket, stamp your hand, the pointing finger
    of a tiny man, beckoning.
You hear the enticing, artificial laugh of the fat lady puppet at the
    "laugh in the dark" ride.


Step right up folks, have some fun, spend your nickel, play some
    games at the Penny Arcade, says the glowing sign in the night.
Dance your cares away at the Dance Pavilion under the crystal ball.
    Glenn Miller melodies are played for all.


Roller coaster, here it comes, be first in line for exciting thrills.
    The many-armed Octopus will spin you round
When the cover descends, you can grab a kiss.
    Don't forget the Bumper cars, they are the best.
There is always a line, so hurry up!

Smells so good, food a-plenty for one and all. Terrific red-hots,

    vinegar fries, barbecue ribs, and yummy mash pies.

Cotton candy on a stick, hand-made waffles with powdered sugar.

    Let's sit down at a picnic table and eat.

We'll go swimming later.


Moms and Dads, and all the kids. Aunts and Uncles, next of kin.

    Very best friends, and sweethearts too,

everyone's here on the Crystal Beach boat at the Canadian pier.


Pay your dollar, enjoy the show, don't get too sunburned or you

    won't sleep tonight.

Drink some Labatt's, Molson's or O'Keefe's, all Canadian brews.

    Hang out with the locals at Jimmy Green's bar.

He's got wonderful fish fries, Blue Pike, fresh from Lake Erie.


Hunker down for a weenie roast, right on the beach. Catch little

    hoppy sand toads, no bigger than a minute, and build a fire.

Roast Aunt Barb's marshmallows and then fall asleep on Mama's lap.

    Dream of the grand tomorrows when you'll be

coming back to Crystal Beach.

## GHOST OF A MOON

She appears, riding high in the clear, late afternoon sky
Her face is ghostly, small, soft as a marshmallow.
Her features won't emerge until darkness envelopes
The still, quiet night.

Now behold her in the blackened silence, in all of her fullness.
A mysterious, ancient, glowing orb, shining, beaming down
Upon us, her constant admirers; needy lovers, all.

The full roundness of her pulsates with love for us.
Our moon comes alive every nightfall, a beauteous bright being
In the emptiness of space.

She pleases all who view this lovely form. We, discerning her
Faithfulness to be there for us always, counting on moon-rise
Forever, unto infinity.

## FALLEN PETALS

Fallen petals, as drops of blood
Shed for love of self.
Put them away forever
Remember them no more.

New life springs from the Geranium
Living, breathing
Soft red petals on my window sill
Dare me to stay
To be brave
To love once more

## TO FORGIVE

To reach out
With my heart and
Accept all things as they are

No wished for dreams
But reality as it is.
My hope is eternal, I hold it close
In my mind and savor it.
I prepare with it for my next
Adventure to come.

## APRIL IN THE VALLEY

Huge, soft, gray marshmallow clouds
    Descend upon the tops of the western mountains.
They roll over thrusting peaks, permeating their low valleys
    Melding with one another.

Heavy and wet, the snow and drizzling raindrops
    Fall on the exposed, naked skin of the mountains.
All shiny and swollen with the liquid love
    Snow blankets the trees and all green things growing.

    April in Antelope Valley.

High, wide, cloud-filled skies. The dark firmament
    Laden with fat, suffocating forms of heavy clouds
Mating with the mountains. At the eastern end
    Of the valley, bright blue skies are filled with
Black birds and ravens all turning somersaults into the wind.

    Nature celebrating Spring.

## FOLIES BERGERE – NEW YEAR'S EVE

The Ray Sinatra orchestra played "Auld Lang Syne" as the old year drew to a close. The audience and the people on stage were hugging and kissing one another as the finale roared to a climax. We were taking our final bows when suddenly a tiny package came sailing over the foot-lights and landed at my feet.

This was followed in quick succession by other packages which various performers picked up, wondering what they were. I opened mine and it contained a one hundred dollar bill, which I quickly tucked inside my costume. I picked up another one that had landed close by. The contents were the same! My friend, Felicia, looked at me and then down at the first row. Sure enough, there sat the Weston brothers, and they were the ones tossing the money onto the stage. They were well known oilmen from Texas and to show their appreciation to us and the cast of the Folies, were rewarding us the best way that they knew how, with money.

"Hey girls, grab all that you can," shouted Gizelle, one of the statuesque showgirls, "It's raining money!" Her tall feathered hat was toppling off of her head as she stooped down to retrieve one of the gifts on the floor. Everyone broke ranks and dived for the packages of money hitting the floorboards. They were coming at a faster pace now and everyone was bumping into one another. I yelled back at Gizelle, "This is almost as good as when Danny D. bought a Cadillac for each of the twelve showgirls at the Sands Hotel. Boy, were they surprised." I spotted a gift next to the trumpet player. "Hurry and get that one before the musicians grab it." She complied, willingly. Felicia ran by me, stuffing money into her ample spangled bra. She said, "I don't think I can hold much more in this tiny costume." Two of the dancers, Bobby and Marie, fell over the parapet but climbed back over quickly before the stage manager could see it. It was pandemonium! Luckily, at that instant, the curtain came down and we exited the stage as the orchestra played furiously to keep the audience happy.

Irene, a topless showgirl, had to put all of her plunder into her brief bikini bottom. As she counted out the bills in the dressing room, she said, "Wow, if ever a finale was great on New Year's Eve, this was the best ever."

# ELAINE E. BROWN

Elaine Brown found her way to the Antelope Valley from her childhood home of Ontario, Canada, where memories of her grandmother reading her children's classics instilled a love of storytelling. She honed her early writing skills by composing letters to friends in distant cities. Later, she juggled raising four children with a career as an Executive Assistant, a position that educated her in the short, tight writing requirements of the engineering field.

Throughout the years Elaine's desire to write fiction grew. She took various creative writing courses, but it was her enrollment in online courses with the LongRidge Writers Group that really pushed her to challenge herself. Now retired, Elaine has more time to devote to writing. She composes short fiction, as well as poetry and haiku, with her co-authors, Mimi and Precious, her two small dogs who are her ever-present desk mates.

## I LIKE TO FIND A PLACE

I like to find a place to sit,
A place upon a rock or beach
Where tumbling thoughts
An order find
And in the finding,
Change the course
Of hellish fantasy and fear.


I like to find a place to trip,
A place of easy passage down
To memories of past times
Where echoes of distant laughter
Float like sea foam
On a rippling breeze.


I like to find a place to crest,
A place transcending current thought.
To soar above the breaking waves
Exploring notions from within
On wings of inspiration.


I like to find a place to run,
A place of space in measured time
Where racing on a track of gold
Unanchored by the chains of doubt,
Thoughts compete with sun to win.


I like to find a place to rest,
A place of vacant solitude
And sail on tranquil tides
To endless blue and endless white
Where thoughts drift silently away.

## NORTHERN BREAKFAST

"Caw! Caw!"

Harsh and strident comes the announcement of the new dawn from high in a distant pine. The night is still almost as black as the raven who heralds the morning. He seems afraid that if he doesn't scream his message loud enough, some poor creature of the forest will oversleep and be late for the affairs of the day.

Cued by nature's alarm clock, the old man rises without hesitation as he has done every day this summer. The others in his family slumber on.

Pulling on his woolen shirt, the old man ambles into the dusky kitchen. After lighting the oil lamp on the table, he fills the black wood stove with firewood and kindling. When he is satisfied that the fire in the woodstove will continue to burn on slowly without his attendance, he begins to gather the items he will need for his early morning adventure.

He takes down the trolling line from its place on the wall, pulls out the small tin pail from the back of the cupboard, and grasps the paddle that is propped in the corner. As he steps out into the rose tinted morning, he is once again filled with the joy of living and the determination to bring back to the breakfast table some of the treasures of the North.

He strides silently toward the beached skiff and gazes out over the calm, glassy lake. Almost as in one motion, he pushes the skiff away from the sandy shore, wipes the night's dew from his seat in the stern, and begins to paddle out around the point, out of view of the log cabin from which he has just come.

Slowly, he unravels the fishing line from the board on which it is wound, letting the silver spinner and three pronged hook with its colorful feather covering drop noiselessly into the depths of the peaceful water. With the fishing line stretched tightly across his knee, and his foot on the board, he continues to paddle with measured strokes and the skill of the old Huron Indian who had taught him years ago.

The tranquility is broken by the persistent tugging of the line against the old man's leg. Careful to keep the line taut, he begins to slowly wind the wet line around the board until the fish, a 20-inch northern pike, is just visible beneath the water. In one motion he lifts and swings the fish over the gunwale and into the center of the boat.

He admires the long, sleek lines of this dark green and black fish as he slides the rope through its mouth and gills. He attaches the rope to the side of the skiff and throws the fish back into the water.

Nearing his destination, he decides not to put the fishing line back into the water until his trip home. He has reached a stretch of shoreline strewn with boulders, deadhead logs, and alder. However, he finds a smooth rock ledge on which to land, and ties the boat securely to a nearby poplar tree.

With tin pail in hand, he cautiously makes his way up toward the granite ridge through the bracken and sumac. He follows the quartz-veined ridge for a short distance until he spots a moss-lined indentation in the rock, well shaded by trees and shrubs. Stooping with the pail between his knees, he begins to deftly lift the plump blueberries from under their green foliage, careful not to disturb the immature white berries.

It has been a good season for the blueberries, and his pail is soon full without the need for further wandering in search of more. He knows he has gathered only enough berries for the family breakfast, but he knows, too, that the family will come here together to pick blueberries for pies and jellies, and to picnic on the shore another day.

Searching out his landmarks, he makes his way back to the skiff. He gently places the pail of berries into a secure spot in the boat and pushes away from the shore, taking his place in the stern and taking up his paddle. Gliding smoothly once again, he follows the shore until he enters a little bay covered with lily pads. He doesn't venture too far within because the water lilies grow densely here.

He stops for a moment to survey the scene. The lily pads remind him somewhat of ladies in white gowns dancing on a green carpet. He decides that three should decorate the table nicely. He pulls on their rubbery stems until they are free, and drops them tenderly into the bottom of his boat.

The sun has moved higher in the morning sky, and the smoothness of the lake is broken by tiny ripples made by the faint beginning of a gusting breeze. He lets out his trolling line again with hopes of another catch or two before rounding the point once more. He is content and much pleased with his treasures for the breakfast table.

But, he knows the greatest treasure of the North is that which rests in his heart, and has become nourishment to his soul. He has found the tranquil peace in the hope of a fresh new day as it leaves behind the dimness of the night. He has felt the harmony and oneness with the awakening nature on this Northern lake.

ELAINE'S HAIKU:

WINTER LACE

Branches spread fingers
Sketching winter lace patterns
On lavender Sky.

## OUT OF SHADOWS

Ghostly shadows, specters on the snow across the reflected lamplight, swallowed the solitary figure. Amy shuffled her footsteps. She obscured their outline on the bitter, cold snow, a diminished and ragged image of her life. Ever vigilant against the unrelenting dangers of the streets, she shifted closer to the dimness by the wall of the cathedral. The faint sounds of organ music drifted about her, mingling with the crystal flakes. She sensed in the moment a small thrill, a vague awakening. This new sensation scared her.

*I should be at the shelter*, she thought, shrinking further into her protective isolation.

She had slipped out of the shelter after the evening meal, drawn by an inexplicable yearning. It was almost Christmas. It had been years since Christmas had held any significance for her except for the small wreath pin, given to her by her mother when she was eleven years old following a children's musical concert in which Amy had participated. Her dreams of a future in music were destroyed when shortly thereafter her father had killed her mother, then himself. Amy, who was always a shy child, withdrew even more. Her life soon revolved around various foster homes. Her reverie took her back to the day she left her last foster home.

"After you get done changing Jamie and packing, you are to come down to the kitchen," Mama Jane demanded of Amy.

Amy changed the sobbing Jamie, hugged him goodbye, and placed him back in his crib. Too many souls torn away from her had splintered and deadened her emotions. With listless hands, she packed her few belongings into her battered suitcase.

"I'm ready, Mama Jane," she said as she entered the kitchen.

Mama Jane, clad in a cotton house dress and cloth slippers, ambled over to where Amy stood against the wall with bent head.

"Now that you are eighteen years old, there is no more money for your support. I don't run a charity here, so you will have to make your own way. I've put some money in this envelope for you," said Mama Jane thrusting the envelope into Amy's hand. She hustled Amy to the door, pecked her carelessly on the cheek, and bid her goodbye. Mama Jane didn't say anything about staying in touch or coming back to visit. There was no thank you for the work Amy had done caring for the younger children since she had finished high school with unremarkable grades. She heard a key turn. Locked out! Put out like a stray cat.

Amy opened the envelope. There wasn't enough for a couple of meals let alone lodging. Amy walked and walked. She cried until tears dried to lead in her heart. Whatever dreams she might have had withered to dust.

Now, five years later, she shivered in the shadows of the cathedral - homeless, loveless, jobless, and surviving on handouts from the shelter and local churches. The sound of Christmas hymns pulled her toward the massive door. Golden light spread across the snow from the door left ajar. Amy slid cautiously inside, pulling her coat closer about her as though to cover her presence here. She edged toward a protective pillar. The music surrounded her. She began to hum softly. Gradually, the music filled her, opened a dark place within her. The music swelled. Released from its prison, her voice soared, reverberating within the arched ceiling.

Slowly, she became aware that the organ music had stopped. In the silence, she heard footsteps approaching. She turned to flee. Too late! A hand gripped her shoulder. Terror overwhelmed her.

"I'm sorry I intruded," Amy stuttered. "Please let me go. I didn't mean any harm."

The man turned her about to peer into her hair draped face. "Miss, your voice!" he exclaimed. "You sound like an angel."

Still cringing, Amy stared in disbelief. "I didn't mean to interrupt, sir."

"Don't worry about interrupting, miss. Please come over to the choir and sing with us." He tugged at her hand, pulling her reluctant figure from the shadow of the pillar. "What's your name, miss?" he asked.

"Amy Cowell, sir," she replied. "I shouldn't be here." She wrung the handkerchief that she clutched as a security blanket, hoping the floor would open up and swallow her.

"No, Miss Amy, stay and sing with us. Don't be afraid. Choir, please help me convince Miss Amy that she is welcome."

The choir smiled as one and clapped their acceptance. Rejection had been her reality for so long that even the approval of the choir frightened her. She tried to slink to the back row. However, the choir master directed her to the front with the sopranos. Music sheets were pressed into her hands. As the music began again, her tension began to thaw. Gradually, she lifted her voice with the choir as they practiced Christmas hymns. Amy felt the magic of these moments of melody fracture the fragile structure of her fortification against a hostile world. When the session was over, she turned to leave. Embarrassment colored her pale face. But the choir surrounded her, lauding her with profuse praise.

The choir master approached, "Miss Amy, I would like to offer you an opportunity to use your wonderful voice, your talent. I want to introduce you to some people who can help you earn a living, maybe launch a very successful career. Will you accept my proposition?"

The promise of a childhood dream, a phoenix from the ashes of her life, was only an agreement away. Dare she reach for it? All of her self-doubts bombarded her. A home of her own, an end to the struggle her life had become. How could she reject his offer? Could she come out of the shadows?

Shyly, she looked up through moist lashes, and reached hesitantly for his outstretched hand.

# JACKIE L. CROSSWHITE SR.

Jackie started writing songs when he was only twelve years old. He was born and raised in Mississippi, and his love of Rock and Roll and Country-western music stems from his Southern roots. He owns the filed copyrights to his many lyrics, some which have been set to music and recorded.

After moving to Southern California, Jackie resided in a number of cities before finally settling his family in the Antelope Valley to enjoy the perfect weather and not-so-crowded living. Retired from the Ford Motor Company, he now enjoys having more time to spend with family, while working as an independent insurance agent. He is still interested in song-writing, but joined the Antelope Valley Writers Association to hone his writing skills. Jackie soon began writing short stories and essays. While still holding on to his dream of having a hit song on the music charts, Jackie has managed to instill his quaint Mississippi country flavor into his prose. He now has a new goal: publishing his memoirs.

## YOU BIG FAT HEAD TURKEY

Gobblers here, gobblers there, gobblers are almost everywhere on old man Jack's farm. My kids call me old man Jack, and it kind of stuck. Anyways, with all of these turkeys running around the place, why in the world am I eating hamburgers for Thanksgiving dinner today?

"What's Thanksgiving without turkey?" everyone is asking. Everybody eats turkey for Thanksgiving. It's been a traditional thing here for hundreds of years. But not today, not this Thanksgiving Day for the fifteen people who are here at my little farm waiting to eat dinner. It's hamburgers or starve.

People tend to compare other people to the turkey bird, insinuating that the bird is stupid, lazy, and just plain don't care. And if someone calls you a big fat head turkey, he probably has a good reason to do so. After you finish reading this story, you can be the judge and decide who is the biggest fat head turkey around here.

In addition to my farm, I have a bar. Now let's go back to my bar two weeks ago. The usual crowd is there, just kicking back, having a few beers, and talking about Thanksgiving and so forth. Some of the people were saying that they had nothing planned for Thanksgiving. Others were saying that they had nowhere to go. I said that the bar would be closed and that I was going to cook myself a big turkey under the ground for about a half of the day. I always cook my goats and turkeys under the ground.

"Boy, the meat just melts in your mouth!" I said, "if anyone wants to come to my house, that's okay. Just bring your own beer and come. But I do need someone to go to my house right now and butcher up two of my turkeys."

Bobby and Bernadette, friends of mine, volunteered to do it if I sent a case of beer along. I did, and they spent four to five hours slaughtering those turkeys. When they finished, they put them in my freezer to keep until Thanksgiving.

Thanksgiving Day comes and I get an early start. I get my fire going in the underground pit; I get my frozen birds out and unwrap them; and I put them right into the pit without checking them. About two hours later, there's a bad odor in the air. My family is saying, "What's that smell?" I just ignore it without trying to find out where it is coming from, figuring that it is probably a brush fire somewhere.

About eleven o'clock the people begin to arrive. The big question from everyone is, "Gee, what's that smell?"

"I don't know. Someone is surely burning something," I answer.

Finally I go out back to the fire pit to check if the birds are ready. Oh my gosh! That's where the smell is coming from. What is wrong? What would cause them to smell like this? So I open that pit and take out the birds. Whew, that's bad! It's got the whole neighborhood stinking.

Then I notice that the birds were never gutted; they still had the intestines and all the other inner parts still in them. I call Bobby and Bernadette over and ask them why they didn't gut the birds. They say that they did not know that the insides had to come out. Now I have birds that the dogs won't even eat.

I had to toss two twenty-five pound turkeys into the trash bin. So this is why I am cooking hamburgers for dinner today. I did not have time to do another turkey.

So who is the biggest fat head turkey of them all? Is it (A): Bobby and Bernadette for not taking the insides out of the birds, or is it (B): me, old man Jack, for not checking out the birds to make sure that they were okay before putting them in the fire pit, or (C): all of the above. You make the call.

## ELLIE

Actually I can't just say Ellie is my pet; I'll have to say Ellie is our pet, because she is the family pet. Most folks have dogs, cats, even mice. But our pet is a female horse, a mare, and she is a registered quarter horse. Her registered name is "Lil Snip Chex," but we know her as "Ellie," which is her barn name.

Ellie was born on February 21, 1984 in Whittier, California. She is 29 ½ years old now, weighs around 1100 pounds, and stands 15.2 hands tall. For non-horse folks, that's 5 feet and 2 inches, measured from the ground to the top of the withers at the shoulder blade. She is a chestnut color, and the two rear legs have white stocking from hooves to the knees. Her left front leg has a stocking from the hoof to the ankle, and she has a little white snip on her forehead just above her nostril. That's how she got her name, L'il Snip Chex.

Ellie's daddy was a registered quarter horse that lived out in Temecula, California. In 1986 he was World Champion in the category, Senior Working Cow, and also second place in Senior Reining categories. In 1987 he was runner-up in both of these classes. The champion that year was also owned by the same people that owned Ellie's daddy. They wanted to breed their champion stallion with our Ellie. Boy, what a blood line that would be! That baby would have a daddy and a grandpa that were back-to-back World Champions in two different categories; it would probably have been worth a half million as soon as it hit the ground, but it never happened. Our Ellie's never been bred in her 29 ½ years.

We got Ellie when she was three years old, and she became just a pet. I broke her to ride. She "rodeoed" with me a few times, but nothing serious. She looks as good now as she did when she was five years old. She's strong, healthy, and still rides. Everyone that sees her still wants to buy her. No, she's not for sale - she's just Ellie, our family pet.

## PARTY PLACE (Song lyrics)

Hey pretty little lady with that big bright smile,
Come on out and let's play for awhile.
We'll go to the park to where our friends are kicking it,
We can go down there and hang out for a bit.
The music is a-popping and a-rocking,
And if you're not having fun then you're not in.
Your mama said stay home you can't go,
But it don't hurt what mama don't know.

The park has something going every Saturday night,
If you love to have fun come check out the site.
We're just having good times we're not doing anything wrong,
Just dancing to the music and now and then sing a song.
My girlfriend and I we come often to party hardy
    and kick up our heels,
But sometimes her mama said no and that's how she feels.
I don't care if mama said no you can't go,
It don't hurt what mama don't know.

We love to play and that's not a sin,
Bring your party partner and jump right in.
You can party all day and into the night,
You'll be safe and sound with security on site.
Come early stay late come all come one,
Join the crowd and let's have some fun.
Your mama may say no that you can't go,
But it don't hurt what mama don't know.

You're only young once you can't turn back the clock,
Get out there and party while you can still rock.
Let the local park be your party site,
Go meet your friends there every Saturday night.
Hey pretty little lady with that big bright smile,
Come on out and let's play for awhile.
I don't care if mama said no you can't go,
It don't hurt what mama don't know.

## THE ANT

Hello, my name is Adam, and I am an ant. I am one of the smallest creatures on Earth, at least that you can see without using a telescope. People call us insects. We live in colonies in the ground, in dead trees, in the walls of humans' houses and buildings, and mostly anywhere there is ample food and water.

My main concern is: what is my purpose of being here on earth? Why did God put ants here? There's got to be reasons why he wanted us on this big, big earth. Well, we're smart and energetic. We have a queen ant to rule each colony. All other ants are workers, soldiers, and builders. We build our own colonies, and we send soldiers and scouts out to look for food and water. We can build a bridge across a stream or river with our bodies so that we can cross to the other side.

Yet, human beings hate us. They spray poison into our homes and nests to kill us. They stomp on us and crush us under their feet. They don't like us to go into their homes to get food and water for our families. We don't eat a lot; we're small. They don't like us to go to their picnics either. They say that we are pests, but we don't mean any harm; we love to eat out, too.

Small animals and insects use us as a food supply. There are even two big animals that are named after us. They are ANTeater and ANTbear, and we are their prime source of food.

We just can't win. Every animal wants to kill us or eat us. So what is the purpose of us being here? I guess God only knows; he created us. So maybe we're here to just be a part of the circle of life. The end

## DREAMING OF DEBBIE

When I was a youngster, my fantasy love was the one and only Debbie Reynolds, the movie actress. She was a cutie, a living doll, and I was head over heels in love with this little hunk of a woman. Even though she starred in lots of movies, I was hung up on the backwoods girl from Mississippi in the *Tammy* movie. I'd seen it over and over, and the more I saw, the deeper I fell in love. I would think, "Man! If I had her for real, I'd be the happiest person in the world."

I knew this was fantasizing, but it did not stop me from dreaming. I kept her living in my world for years and she never knew it. "Oh Tammy, oh Tammy," I would walk around singing her theme song, "I love you so." Believe me, this was no play acting; I was serious. I kept living in her world for years and she never knew it.

I'm very sincere about Debbie. When I first saw her smile my heart surrendered completely. I kept praying that I would have her some day. The thrills kept growing on and on. When I'd see a falling star I'd start dreaming of Debbie. If I could hold her in my arms, that would be heaven to me. If I could kiss her I would feel like a king. She would make my life complete and I would never let her go. I couldn't help being in love with Debbie, my fantasy.

How long can I pretend? She's everything a girl should be and everything a man could want, but she's not mine for real, and it still breaks my heart. Some say that I'm a fool, so be it. I'll be that fool. I can't stop loving her. I've loved her much too long, so I'll live my life in dreams and memories. I will not stop believing. I will hold on to my feelings forever, treasuring my eternal devotion to Debbie. People said that Mr. Franklin could not catch electricity in a bottle, but he did. They said that Mr. Bell could not talk over a wire, but he did. They said a man could not walk on the Moon, but he did.

Who knows? Someday I may go to Las Vegas, walk in to a casino where she is performing, go to her dressing room and just walk right in without knocking and say, "Debbie, I've come to take you home with me." And then she'll say, "What took you so long, Jack? I've been waiting for you for sixty years!"

## PERFECT LOVE
(Song lyrics)

We were meant for each other from the first day that we met.
I don't know where you came from
    but I know that I will never forget.
You were standing there in all of your glory
    looking like an Angel from the Heavens of blue.
That's when you fell in love with me and I fell in love with you.

They say that true love only comes once in a life time
    and I believe that is true.
I know that you were God sent to me
    and that I was God sent to you.
Oh baby look into my eyes and tell me that you love me
    and that you will always be mine.
And I'll see sweetness in your eyes as I tell you
    that I will love you till the end of time.

We'll go to the church and see the preacher man.
And we'll get married as soon as we can.
We'll promise our love to each other in the eyes of our God above.
Then we will know that our love is pure and that it's a perfect love.

# LA RUE ALEGRIA

La Rue was born on the southwest coast of Texas. Her family's origins are from Oklahoma with Native American roots. She traveled much with her family due to her father's career in the military, but has called the Antelope Valley her home for the past twenty-five years.

Her love of writing began in middle school, where she took up journaling. She continued to write while living in Hawaii, where she fell in love with writers of poetry - Edgar Allen Poe, Robert Lewis Stevenson, Robert Frost – and was inspired by Frost's "The Road Less Traveled."

La Rue was later encouraged to continue writing by her younger daughter. She devoted two years writing with a Free Writers Group on the Internet, where her fellow writers urged her to never stop. She found additional inspiration from authors such as Natalie Goldberg, who wrote *Writing Down the Bones* and *Wild Mind*; Anne Lamott's *Bird by Bird*; and Julia Cameron's *The Artist's Way* and *Morning Pages Journal*.

La Rue is also an artist who has had her work on tour of the U.S. for eight years, exhibiting at Kennedy Center for the Arts, and Harvard, Princeton, Yale, and Vanderbilt Universities. She has been published in the public domain through John Wiley and Sons, New York, New York.

## GUMBO SHRIMP

He was like a Gumbo Shrimp of a Man
A man or a beast? A beastly man, I did not know
Most times he was pretty nice
upon our first encounter with one another
Mama's first official date
with him and us three kids in tow

Out to dinner it was quite late for such an early hour
Gray outside with spring showers

I was acting natural, as I sat like a toy in the back seat

Of the Army Green old Dodge
That looked like it once belonged to General Patton

I was deeply superficial,

unseen to the human eye

extremely happy,

but in great agony
grief and sorrow...

The acceptance of this Gumbo Shrimp of a Man
Was more important to me than a little eight year old

Could wrap her mind around

He was pretty ugly most of the time

He was going to be my new Dad?

Always trying so hard to win the Gumbo Shrimp of a Man's award,
but the beast in him would always arise
A beastly man at first I did not know, we all sat down to eat bowls

Of Shrimp Gumbo....

## LOVE YOURSELF LIKE A ROSE

How would you treat a Rose
Would you treat it like a precious gift
Would you crush it
Would you force it into a vase

Would you tear the petals off
without any thought or care or grace
Would you cut it,

leave it
out of the water to quickly fade

This is how we are not to treat ourselves
We must treat ourselves like the lovely Rose
Multicolored in nature and beauty
With tantalizing smells
Velvet skinned petals
Strewn where brides walk the aisles

A Red Rose is the creative spirit of love
True love much stronger than its thorns of death
Cardinal red, sublime desire
Fire Red, flames of passion
If you should buy yourself some of them
You may find that spark,

that reminder to treat yourself
with love

Yellow Roses are for friendship
Domestic Bliss,
Sympathy
Can we do none the less for ourselves
than to live out what the Yellow Rose means

The White Rose, loyalty
 Loyalty to ourselves
Able to captivate secret thoughts
A flower of secret love

White Rose of Confession
The Rose of the Bride
Rose of Servitude
Let us love and nurture ourselves

Pink Rose, Grace, elegance, refinement
and sweeter than sweet thoughts
Gentleness, and kindness we give to ourselves

Purple Rose can be showy
of enchantments and Transcendence
Opulence, Majesty, Purple is for Kings
and Queens for those of Royalty

The meaning of the Orange Rose
is that I am proud of you
we should wear them on our vests
on our heads
sprinkle their petals upon our beds

Blue Roses, yes it's true there is a Blue Rose
It's not just for the blues
It's fantasy and Impossibility
Hoping for Miracles and new possibilities
Many bloomed in the Orient

The Black Rose, *Les fleurs du mal*
from which beauty springs.
Sometimes a beautiful deep red rose
will bloom from a blackened bud.
Remember no matter what may come or go
treat yourself like the Rose.

Bask in the majesty and the beauty of oneself.

## CRYSTAL STREAMS OF LONG AGO

Red man danced on Mother Earth's Red Soil
Stomp dance, war dance, rain dance too
The Red soil was Mother Earth's Womb

Every step was a prayer in the dance
For all the ancestors that have gone on before us
For all that are with us, and those yet to be born

White man stole our land
Stole our way of life
Living under the stars
Fishing in the clear crystal streams
Walking in the meadows

Hearing the Meadowlarks sing

Wearing our buckskins, covered by Buffalo hides at night

Sleeping under the shadow of the Almighty Wings
Eagles fly in the night while we sleep in peace and safety

We were content to get by, Mother Earth she provided

She loved us too much to starve us

We fought the cold bitter winter snows
Huddled up in our teepees

Mother had painted scenes of nature upon the teepee walls
She made a fire when we were cold
Shadows danced upon those walls
Of Crystal Streams in our dreams of long ago

### FIGHT OR FLIGHT OF LIFE I'VE RAN AGAIN

Good to hear from you, you fiery little horny devil you... Just got back from the coast. Was at a hotel with a natural hot spring...

Huge suite with a jacuzzi bath tub as big as a train. Put way too many bubbles in it though. Got lost in all the suds. Then took off two days later for the beach. Stayed in a hotel, the only one on the whole beach, very, very "south of the border" motif, to go with the tiny beach cove town. The inner courtyard had a huge old wagon full of baskets of flowers, and some wonderful cane rocking chairs with huge metal yellow suns on their backs, with vibrant cobalt blue metal trim....the day was glorious, sat on the beach in the warm California sun, a V.I.P beach hardly anyone there...This coastal town has the *Diablo Diobolic*, Nuclear Power Plant right next to it...I laughed to myself, well if any nukes go off while I am here I will be glowing dust on the beach...I sat and worked on my old frayed worn out quilt patching its frayed grandmother fans. I had bought this multicolored red, blue, green, yellow, white quilt at an antique mall several years ago for my birthday. An artist friend of mine was with me, I surveyed the stitching on the quilt, the stitches were a mess. I told her hey, look here at this stitching, either a challenged person put this quilt together or someone who was blind. Found plastic pop can material sewn into the patches. Far away it looked really pretty, ah but close up that was another story. I guess you could say kind of like when a guy is at the bar and he's had too many drinks and the gal across the room really looks good...I bought it simply because who ever pieced it and quilted it gave it their best shot. I thought that is similar to our lives.

Our lives can look so together from far away but close up 'egads!' we can downright scare one another, huh? Yep, and at times even scare ourselves...

But that is just the point, the point is Unconditional love. We love one another warts and all, bad stitches and all, we are a patchwork of many patterns, (moods) and colors (feelings) and the work itself, how it was put together doesn't really matter does it? The main thing is that we are here...We belong, bad stitching and all...That quilt has brought me great warmth and comfort for many long years now... Our lives can bring warmth and comfort to those around us...God has us here for a purpose.

I moseyed over to the Sycamore Natural Springs Spa and stayed the night. Floated in the nude in the spa outside the door of my room. Floating there in my birthday suit felt so free, it reminded me of what it must have been like being in that warm hot womb with a view... I soaked, and ate wonderful healthy gourmet meals, and soaked some more, and drank wines from the local coastal vineyards, and slept and dreamt sweet dreams. Had a massage today before I left and was so relaxed I fought sleep driving the five hour drive home. My eyes kissed the green hill sides dreading coming back to the desolate desert.

I felt as if I had saw dust packed in my chest pressed down and shaken together and running over out of my soul, the corners of my eyes, as the green hills descended behind my rear view mirror...to the brown rugged hillsides of the grapevine...The grapevine is a huge highway that travels up and over a huge pass from Bakersfield to Los Angeles. It was raining, and windy, I looked to my left and saw the most massive brightly colored rainbow I have seen in years. I teared up, it was so glorious. I pulled over and took a picture of it, I just could not pass it up... I wondered to myself where do I belong on this Earth plane?

Someone told me once that we are exactly where God wants us to be at this given moment in time...we are in fact exactly where we are supposed to be, doing what it is we are doing. But I must cut to the chase...even if this is truth...I cannot deny how I truly feel... I hate the desolation of the desert, is it due to how it makes me feel, or does it only accentuate how I already feel? But how can that be when I am away I get so renewed and refreshed?

Must be my frame of mind.

I am working on the back yard for the spring. I have put a new spa in, and plants, and some Italian Cypress, and mirrors I have embellished with sea shells, pearls, and beach glass, going to paint the cement block wall with scenes of green shutters overlooking a cove at the beach, like the very beach I sat at working on my quilt. If I can't be at the coast at this time in my life, while I am waiting for that to transpire, I will bring the coast to me... LOL. I am going to do great Spanish archways with lots of lush Bougainvillea vines and Fuchsia flowers everywhere, and graceful palms with their wonderful burlap trunks and luscious pond fronds... Maybe a Macaw or two, and of course a Parrot I must have a parrot...The tropics are calling me...

Must be the erotica that erupts inside of me when I feel the warm sun and sand on my skin...

I am just a lover of nature, a lover of the one who made all the glorious beauty all around us...a horny lover of God...lover of my soul who delights in making things beautiful for me his daughter... I am an artist I am only his copy cat...

# ERIKA HAWKINS

Erika Hawkins moved to the Antelope Valley from Chicago, Illinois and is one of the original members of the Antelope Valley Writers Association. She studied writing at Los Angeles City College, and has a realist approach to her poetry, which is sometimes raw and at other times humorous. She has a style that is reminiscent of famous African-American poets like Gwendolyn Brooks. Yet, Erika has developed a unique writing flavor that is all her own.

She is also a deft storyteller and her stories have made it into various literary anthologies. Erika is currently publishing a collection of her short stories which will be on the marketplace by Christmas 2013, in both print and eBook format.

## KANGAROO JONES

Under a Vanilla Sky
rabbit minds will surely find on the podium
of the grateful dead, angels' wings laid to rest.

Reigning on a myriad of savannahs about the
women's loins. Before butterflies,
after Beulah Land, in crew cut,
on mesa head, under sympathy.

With a music of tambourines, jingling like the
play-off of no tomorrow.
Yellow-tailed feathered hats appraised to the
tune of,

"I'll fly away Ole' Glory, I'll fly away!"

Birds words, outside crooning, child's play
whilst Sunday blares another hour of peaceful
power.

Blessedness, Blessedness!
The choir blares on the second floor of Heaven.

## RUBBA DICE

He threw into the air thrice.

Closing all doors onto the table's scores.

The House against him. His drawers were filled
like diamonds' eyes.

The Magic was tragic. One-win, two-win, where
to begin, or where to end. Gold thrown up
onto the air, in animated suspension. Old snake
eyes, double-betted by surprise. Snapped his
fingers for the dead-ringer.

Dice rolled out of his mouth, he cajoled,
"Come on eights lay pretty for me.
This is for Lily, baby."

The House hushed. The dice rushed, and hit Eight.

Lord, you could hear Heaven's pearly gates.
All betters were on his side, the game did not
remain the same.

The House handed each one dollar chips,
to the tune of hundreds. Then came the
martini sips. Some jubilant screams, his hands shook
when he blew the dice. "Give me one mo' big
Dream."

## THE PENTHOUSE BITCH

I'd like to live in high-rises like Eliza's
and Malaysia's

Eating that candle-lit dinner, telling me I'm
the only eventual winner

While lover's at home

I sit by the telephone alone,
waiting for hiz call

Ring-a-ling a ling. Hello, bellows a hoarse voice
from late night fright

Anybody for a sick treat some live meat?

## AMBIGUITY

Within the law of confusion,
I often ask myself,

What comprises the results of Ambiguity?

Why should it exist, anyway?
For this day, or any day in the near future
no answers may I obtain, unless it's a Dr. Seuss's

Lawyer, who surprises me, stating factually,
"No crisis for thee,
Everything is hunky-dory"

Deep down I know the key.
Would you celebrate with me?

Ambiguity

What would I do without him?
Can you telepathically call the Lord's
dictionary for me, and come up with sound
evidence to represent the real case, to the face
of justice?

Or is the premise too bold for words?
Never to neglect what the Lord gives to the victim?

## MISTER REYNOLDS

Getting lost was very easy. Staying on target was the hard part, in her rented car, trying to find a room for one. She didn't want what one would call Re-hab or Transitional. After speaking to her on the phone, she remembered the lady said, "Avenue P-10." God, she thought it's got to be somewhere near here.

The sun was aggravating. Just beginning to penetrate the glorious heated morning warmth, which seeped through the car's window. One more block and there would be the street. She'd made it on a full tank of gas. She saw the canal, a beautiful aqua-marine reservoir. She thought about jumping in for a ten-minute bath. She had the soap, the best Irish Spring, sitting in the glove compartment of the rental car.

Crossing the railroad tracks, she smelled dung from one of her favorite species of animal, a horse. Hiding conspicuously behind the veil of a small wooden sign, there it was, Avenue P-10. It truly reminded her of the old Western ghost town days, which she perceived to be a good thing. She turned and then veered to the right, worrying about the rental car's tires picking up rusty nails from the dirt road. She saw grassy mountains, sitting right smack dab in the middle of nowhere, and surrounding what would be her future room. Sitting and aging along the road were Yucca trees that carried cactus milk, and people said the leaves could be eaten.

Excited, she exited the car, placing her keys in her new red leather purse. She walked up the stairs of the small trailer and knocked. Immediately she knew she could afford something like this. A leprous woman answered, followed by a trail of beautiful Collies. She entered and the blonde-haired, blue-eyed lady invited her to sit on an old sofa infested with dog hair. They discussed the price of the room, which was agreeable. She didn't have much, just a few clothes in an attaché case she'd picked up from the five and dime store.

The kitchen, bath, and bedroom all needed severe attention; they looked as if a dust bowl blew a cyclone through the vestiges of the walls and carpets. For three weeks it was learning, and cooking, and running from the leprous woman's dogs. The lady's trust became confident. So, on this particular Saturday, she decided to leave for the neighborhood feed store for hay.

"A remarkable diet," said the roomer.

"No, it isn't for me, it's for my horses."

She nonchalantly fluffed off the imaginary tales the lady proposed to arouse her interest, and decided to mind her own business. She turned soldierly toward her room. But after listening for the car to whistle down the road, something inspired her to check out the surroundings outside. She did have the keys to the front door. She let herself out and waded around the perimeter of the property, all alone. There were no dogs to protect her; they weren't that friendly to her anyway. Her head was in deep thought as she walked along the light brownish earth, glimpsing the rising sun on the mountains.

She walked like a blind woman, not knowing what lay before her. In front was a fence of sturdy steel. In the corner, behind the tin-roofed yard were bales of hay. This led her to believe that behind the corral were horses. She was in her bare feet and wore a dress three sizes too big, and instinct told her not to get any closer. She'd read of instances where people were mauled for getting too close to strange animals. Curiosity overwhelmed her instinct, as she walked closer to the enclosed yard and neighed like a horse. Out of the entrails of the tin roof appeared a wild buck with ragged hooves and skeletal ribs protruding through the veins of his hungry stomach. Yet he managed to lure her to the fence. His face was worn with years of sorrow and his eyes and teeth smiled a yellow hue.

The first thing to enter her mind was to find food. Anything at this point. She ran as fast as she could back to the trailer. In the kitchen she opened all the cans of carrots and gathered some apples. Time was ticking. What if the leprous lady caught her? Sympathy abounded for the poor old horse and she left the carrots and apples, then hurried back into the trailer to retreat to her room before the lady returned from the store. She would act as if she'd seen nothing, knew nothing. She could feel the horse eating hastily, and she began to hum nervously around her room.

The day waned, the sore sun beamed, and so did her physical energy. She decided to chance going to the corral. There lying on the earthen floor was that horse. She turned in awe – feeling depressed, scared, and guilty. Flies were surrounding the horse's body. But as she turned to run back to her room, miraculously the horse stood on all fours. She jubilantly turned around to face him, smiling and rubbing the top of his head as the horse approached her at the corral and neighed, "My name is Mr. Reynolds."

# MELINDA M. HUNTER

Melinda M. Hunter, a recent transplant to the Antelope Valley, is from Oak Park, Illinois. She is an active member of the Antelope Valley Writers Association, and she now calls the "high desert" her home. Melinda has a B.A. degree from Carleton College in English, and holds an M. Div. degree from North Park Seminary. She has one son, John Emerson Hunter, who also lives in the Antelope Valley.

Blessed with an amazing talent, she is able to recite from memory poetry that she wrote as a child. She has been writing poetry since she was five. Melinda also enjoys writing Haiku and short stories, particularly using animals as her characters. Currently she is working on a story about her cat, Oro.

MELINDA'S HAIKU:

## FLIGHT

The bird's nest is empty.
The young striped fledglings
Have flown away.

## CAT

On red tile roof
Cat lies
Suns himself.

## SILVER MOON

Silver moon
Plays peek-a-boo
Behind lacey, cloud curtain.

## TO AN INSECT ON MY WINDSHIELD

With translucent wings and slender white legs

You appear on my windshield.

So delicate that you could be crushed instantly

But I am inside the car and you are outside.

I almost pull over to assist you.

Fly, little pretty wings, fly, I urge.

Distracted for a minute, I look down.

When I look again, you are gone,

Blown away by a gust of wind.

## TWISTED TREE

I saw a twisted tree

outside the Cultural Center.

It curved left

in a close to perfect angle.

A tree, misshapen,

but full of beauty.

Its pink blossoms fill the air

With color and scent.

I saw a twisted boy

outside the Cultural Center,

his back bowed in a hump.

A youth, misshapen,

but full of beauty.

He is a gift from God filled with

life and promise.

## WALMART AT NIGHT

It's amazing what you see

In Walmart at night:

A homeless man,

Whose hair, beard and clothes

Are the same shade of khaki,

Covered with dirt.

A young black man who comments,

"I like your toes," painted red with a flower on the big toe.

(Made my evening)

A very large woman in a motorized shopping cart,

Her basket filled to the rim with potato chips, sugary pop, and ice cream.

A harried Mom, with five kids in tow, some white, some black, one Hispanic,

A 16-year old couple, arms entwined, kissing.

An older woman with a long gray braid, buying some frozen dinners and canned soup.

"America the Beautiful. "

Some look happy, some look sad, some are in a hurry, some are lonely.

But all are here together in Walmart on Saturday night.

## DRACTICFALACTICS

Dracticfalactics are strange looking things,
They resemble a rabbit with crocodile wings.
Their eyes are the color of a hen's front teeth,
And around their necks is a striped wreath.

Well as I was saying 'bout Dracticfalactics,
They have no money and very few tactics.
Why when I was up in Kalamazoo,
They saw the Mayor and they all said, "Boo!"
His very white face turned a purplish red
And the top just blew right off of his head.

On burned up orchids this strange beast dines,
On boiled or stewed curtains and squares, holes, and lines.
And on Saturday night at a quarter of nine
He buys watermelons and chews up the rinds.

Well I hope you have learned from my wonderful poem
That when it gets dark you had better stay home.
Dracticfalactics are beasts to respect.
When they are around, watch out for your neck!

## POURING

My life is defined by pouring.

I pour the coffee beans into the grinder then

Pour the ground coffee into the filter to make coffee.

I pour dry cat food into a dish

To feed my cats.

I pour the bird feed into the feeder

To feed the hungry birds.

I pour myself into the lives of others

To bring comfort, peace and relief from pain.

I turn to God when I am empty

To fill me up so I can pour again.

## DESIRE

It is as if
By staring at the computer screen
I could force you to respond to me.

But there is no response.

Over a week ago
You invited me to your room,
Asked me to stay,
Kissed me and held me
And aroused my desire.

I didn't stay.

But the incident has seared my memory,
And brought back scenes from the past
Where I was deeply hurt.
I have no claim on you,
Nor you on me.
I want to drop this
And move on.

I wrote.
You wrote back.
I wrote again (twice)
Perhaps too intensely.
The second time
I tried to explain
Which never works.

I need to let go
And turn this over to God.

# JOSE GALLO

Jose "Jessie" Gallo combines his personal experiences of working in the culinary industry with his writing. After spending his high school years building up work experience in restaurant kitchens, Jessie enrolled and received his degree at the Le Cordon Bleu College of Culinary Arts in Pasadena, California. While at Le Cordon Bleu, he discovered his love of writing and became an active writer with the school's newsletter, *Mirepoix*.

Currently, he spends his days freelancing for catering companies while working at a local sushi restaurant, and continues to develop his writing skills as a member of the AVWA. Besides using his talent as a writer and a cook to compose stories of his behind-the-scenes culinary experiences, Jesse wants to eventually produce a book in the graphic novel genre.

## LATIN HERITAGE

"In the domain of the Del Valle kitchen, my mother is the dictator. I refer to it as Carmen's culinary queendom; she becomes a cuisine *conquistadora* wielding a freshly sharpened knife like a sword above her head." - Mayda Del Valle

---------------

Growing up within a Latin home it is very common to have an overcritical family that has a strong cooking heritage. In a way it is a part of our identity, having home-made recipes passed on from generation to generation. For us, food is a celebration that brings the family closer together. Using manteca to make sancocho, pupsusas, menudo, and huevos rancheros, and as it fills the air with a sense of appreciation, you take the time to enjoy it all.

Yes, our food is high in fat and you will gain two pounds when you finish eating, but it is the fat that gives it a lot of flavor and makes it taste so good. It's something that brings pleasure to your senses with the sweet taste, the tender aroma, the crispy texture, and the beautiful colors that overlap with each other. And it's something I came across everyday at home. Having food with arroz and frijoles is something that is expected with your meal.

Seeing my mom cooking in her tiny kitchen to make the family a feast at every family gathering, and helping her make enchiladas is something that shaped me into the cook I am today.

## THE TEQUILA INCIDENT

In life we come across these moments. Moments, that when they occur, we don't realize that they are life-changing.

One such moment started with the impulse to mimic a chef on television. I remember sitting on the couch in the house all to myself, doing nothing but watching television to escape my boredom. That was until hunger hit me. Now being a child of the 90's, I didn't want to wait for my parents to come home to make me something to eat. So I did what any sensible seven year old kid would do; I looked at the television for answers. As I flipped through the channels, I saw a man preparing sautéed chicken. I remember seeing him flambé a chicken to create a little fire and thought, "That's so cool! I want to try that!"

Grabbing everything from the fridge, I began to mimic the television chef with every step. I heated the pan with oil, hearing the fat spark and crackle in the air. Then I cut leftover chicken, onions, and garlic into bite size pieces, trying not to make myself cry as I tossed it all into the pan. The food sizzled. As the chicken began to brown, I could smell the sweetness of the onion and the sharpness of the garlic come together, creating an aroma that my little Einstein dictionary couldn't describe.

Everything was going well, except when it came time to add the wine, the very thing I needed to create the little fire. As I searched and searched, I quickly found out that we didn't have any. My family wasn't the type to buy wine. So I checked every pantry I could reach, for something else I could use. Luckily, I came across a bottle of high proof tequila. Thinking wine and tequila were the same I went ahead and poured the entire bottle straight into the pan. Looking back on it now, I shudder at the mistakes I made in preparing that dish. But no one would have cared that the chicken was a bit under seasoned, since the fire was on full blast, and I didn't know how strong tequila really was.

In a moment an enormous fire erupted from the pan, catching me by surprise and knocking me back. The blaze just petrified me.

All I could think was, "Oh my god, oh my god, I'm gonna burn the house down and my parents are gonna kill me."

Not knowing what to do, I panicked and tried to blow out the massive fire with my child sized lungs. I kept blowing and blowing with all my might until finally the flame died out on its own. With the food now burnt to a crisp and my life shortened by several years. I saw my hands were shaking tremendously. Still, all I could say was, "That was cool."

## SPANISH RISOTTO

Within my home I constantly find myself, an individual who has been trained to prepare various dishes from around the world, at odds with my family. They are a group of people who are very prideful of their Latin heritage, and they are territorial when it comes to the food we prepare at home.

With all my experience working at several different restaurants, catering companies, and the occasional self-catered event, I have had the opportunity to meet a wide array of people. Each has their own set of quirks, preferences, and even plans to take over the world. However, never in my life have I met anyone who has driven me so insane as my family does in the kitchen. Every time, and I mean every time, I try to cook something that isn't of Mexican origin, my family feels compelled to intervene.

"Mijo, you're doing it wrong."

"No mom, I'm not."

"Mijo why are you stirring it? When you're cooking rice you're suppose to leave it alone."

"Mom, I'm not making arroz, I'm making risotto. It's completely different."

"Now you're adding vino?!"

"Yes! That's how you're supposed to prepare it."

"Mijo, step aside. I'll show you how you're supposed to cook arroz."

"Of course, Mom. I have no idea what I'm doing. It's not like I spent two years going to culinary school to cook professionally. Oh wait I did!"

## BONDS

Within the culinary realm, cooks, chefs, and all pursuers of good cuisine develop a bond that is forged through shared hardships within the kitchen. This bond is something that many do not understand and mere words cannot do it justice. And this is something that I share with my fellow colleague and friend Sean.

"I'm gonna kick your ass."

"I think you mean 'kiss your ass', and yes you are."

"I will hurt you."

"I heart you too."

"Give me a good reason why I shouldn't shove my foot so far up, for convincing me to get up at 4:00 AM, take an hour long train to meet up with you, for us to cook for fifteen hours straight on my only day off."

"I'll buy you Starbucks when you get here."

"Okay we're good then."

Now I know that our friendship may seem strange, but there is something about cooking for hours on end that gives us those traits. That cynical sense of laughter we get, whenever someone mentions that they'll be making over forty grand a year. Or the instant connection and understanding we make with complete strangers whenever we talk about the shit storm that we feel in the thirty minute window to serve salads, appetizers, and the main dinner for a party of five hundred people.

I recommend you work in a kitchen to see how the people interact with one another, if you ever want to understand the strangeness of these bonds.

## UNEXPECTED CONSEQUENCES

In the two years I spent in culinary school, I've found myself in many situations that had me view things differently. One such event occurred shortly after my Food Safety and Sanitation class. There I was shown the horrors of poor kitchen management that made me paranoid of Salmonella, Botulism, and cross contamination, just to name a few recurring nightmares I have since I chose this profession.

Since then, when I found myself with food after each class, I couldn't take it home with me because at the time I didn't have a car. And that would mean leaving food at room temperature for about two and half hours. Now coming from a Latin home, I was taught that food is very precious and shouldn't be thrown away. Instead, I began to give the food away to various random people on my way to the train that would take me home. This of course made me popular with the local shopkeepers, the homeless, and the train station workers who would double check the train just to make sure I was there in order to get some free food.

However, things got really interesting during my advance baking and dessert classes. I made things like bite size strawberry and kiwi fruit tarts, chocolate truffles, apple crisps with oat toppings, or the ever popular layered cakes. One such cake was a flourless chocolate cake that was repeatedly stacked with strawberry mousse, cake, more mousse, and more cake. I finished it with a chocolate coating that formed a crunchy shell with strawberry chips placed on top. Now because of my talent with desserts, I had built up a certain reputation that attracted many people. One in particular stood out.

One day at Union Station where I was walking towards my train ride home, a girl with fiery red hair ran up in front of me, pulled me by the collar close to her, and asked, "Are you the chef who's giving out free cake to random strangers?" Because it happened so fast, I couldn't find the words to speak; all I could do was present her with a strawberry short cake. And that is how I met my girlfriend.

INDEPENDENCE

Whenever I stand before an empty kitchen, I start to wonder what I can do with it.

For as long as I can remember, I have always had to abide by someone else's rules regarding the kitchen. Their methods, their techniques, their ways of thinking were something I always had to adapt to in every kitchen I've ever worked in. It was their kitchen. Even if I disagreed with their methods, it was their way, no exception. As I began working and learning from various chefs at the different jobs I had accumulated over the years, I started to think about how I wanted to run my own kitchen in the event that I somehow managed to open up my own business.

If you ever get a chance to see a chef in action within their own kitchen, I highly suggest you take the time to watch them operate. The way everything is set into place, how they move about the kitchen, and what sort of ingredients they have laying around is a reflection of who they are. As for myself, I have always operated with logic, practicality, and creativity within the realms of my own limitations. Some cooks have the desire to own a four star, high quality kitchen where every small detail is considered to be a work of art, but I have never been attracted to that side of the industry. My perfect place would be a cafe. Nothing fancy or big, but simple and welcoming. A place with an open kitchen where I could interact with the people in a small residential neighborhood outside of the city.

When I think about what the actual cafe would look like, I often picture the Furakawa Bakery as seen in an old Japanese cartoon series called *Clannad* that I used to watch. It is a bakery that doubles as a home, where the cafe is neatly displayed in front while the personal home is located behind and on top of it. From the moment I saw that bakery, I became attracted to it. Not only because the owners were kind and welcoming but because it has a certain atmosphere where you could be yourself and be at ease. That is the ideal kitchen I someday hope to have.

# WILMA WEBSTER

Wilma Webster is both a scholar and a world traveler. At UCLA, she majored in Near Eastern Studies, and then spent the next fifteen years living in Mexico where she studied Medicine. Wilma returned to the U.S. and worked as an emergency physician for sixteen years, and became involved in writing as editor of Columbia County Medical Society medical bulletins.

With a desire to travel, she joined the Army Reserves and was immediately sent to Saudi Arabia to provide medical services during the Gulf War (Desert Storm). That was followed by eight more years in the Air Force serving in Japan, England, and Panama, as well as in the United States. She continued to write, composing medical articles for the base newspaper. She consolidated her articles into *Wellness Wisdom*, a medical booklet that was issued by the base to new personnel. Retirement from the military did not slow her ambition. She returned to college and earned masters degrees in HR and Psychology.

Wilma has honed her writing skills by composing numerous medical articles and booklets, and editing a monthly newsletter. She now calls upon her diverse background and experiences to write an amazing collection of stories that will eventually become her memoirs.

## FORTY-FIVE MINUTES IN AN AMBULANCE
(A Hospital Experience)

Medical school in Mexico is all but free for Mexican citizens (and foreigners who support Mexican citizens). I had lived in Mexico for thirteen years and was supporting my own two Mexican-born children while going to Medical school at UNAM (*Universidad Nacional Autónoma de México*) in 1973. I paid only about $30 per semester! The catch is that once you finish Medical School, you owe one full year of service to the Mexican government, receiving only a relatively small stipend for your work.

I finished the first four years and then a year of undergraduate rotating internship (when interns spend a month or so working in each medical discipline: cardiology, urology, dermatology, etc.). Once that is accomplished everyone waits for the UNAM lottery to determine where each new doctor will go for *Servicio Social*, with higher achieving students going first.

When it was my turn, I went down the list of open spots with my boyfriend, who spotted with certain excitement, the town of *San Juan del Río* in the State of *Queretaro*. He immediately told me to choose that one because it's a tourist spot for Mexican nationals, and well-known for its delightful atmosphere and thermal water swimming pools.

Soon my two little sons and I had packed everything into our car and were off to our new life in *San Juan,* as we called it for short. We rented an apartment on the main thoroughfare and proudly learned our new address: *Avenida Juarez, No. 12, San Juan Del Río, Queretaro.*

*San Juan* was a small, quaint town when I did social service there in 1978. It had cobblestone streets, beautiful churches and only one stop light in the center of town, which continuously flashed yellow. In true small-town fashion, people would gather frequently here and there at street corners, or wherever they chose, to discuss the latest news.

Instead of front yards, the outer walls of homes were flush with the sidewalk, giving more intimacy for the family inside, but there was invariably a central courtyard graced with bougainvillea, lilies, and geraniums and perhaps a few birds chirping in cages.

After meeting the hospital director, an affable and breathtakingly handsome young physician, I felt much less anxious about my assignment. Two other female doctors, also doing their social service, would alternate shifts with me to maintain 24-hour coverage of a small (9-bed, 3-crib) clinic and hospital. There was an ambulance with a driver to transfer critical patients, if needed, to the regional hospital 45 minutes away in *Queretaro City*, the capital of the state of the same name. Off-duty doctors could be called to fill in for the on-duty doctor during emergencies.

I began work at the San Juan clinic and hospital with a certain amount of trepidation, but quickly settled into a comfortable routine. Patients came in with flu, pneumonia, lacerations in need of repair, broken bones in need of casts, children with diarrhea or "worms," something I had never seen in the United States but that freaked me out in Mexico. A mother would typically bring in the soiled diaper, open it up and say, "My baby did this!" showing me a diaper full of live, writhing worms 6-8 inches long! Where I worked, that usually meant *Ascaris* (roundworms). We had plenty of medication to give out for that along with the usual lecture about washing hands before eating and after going to the bathroom, because *Ascaris* is usually transmitted by fecal contamination from one person to another.

We also saw a number of men who wanted venereal disease (VD) ruled out the day after visiting the local house of ill repute. But what we did most of all at our small clinic/hospital in *San Juan del Río* was deliver babies. The mothers would typically come in with little or no prenatal care and after labor had already begun. Having already delivered over 100 babies during my undergraduate internship, I felt comfortable delivering more.

When a woman in labor would come in, after taking her history and vital signs, I would put her on a bed with stirrups, don a pair of gloves and feel how dilated the uterine cervix was. If it was only an inch or so, I could let her relax in a bed for a few more hours while we monitored her, or send her home to wait longer if she lived nearby. When delivery seemed imminent, I'd proceed with the delivery.

Usually pregnancies and deliveries go well with or without a doctor. The baby comes out normally, head first, and goes through the normal positional changes as it traverses the birth canal. Doctors are really only needed in childbirth for those few times when there is fetal or maternal suffering, such as in *Eclampsia*, when the mother's blood pressure goes sky-high, putting both her baby's and her own life in danger.

Other doctor-required situations are: when the umbilical cord is tightening around the baby's neck, or in the case of *placenta previa* (a poorly positioned placenta blocking the baby's exit and which often leads to severe hemorrhage), or if the baby gets stuck on its way out.

We always listened to the baby's heartbeat with a special Pinard stethoscope, shaped kind of like an hourglass. We would put the Pinard stethoscope on the woman's belly and our ear directly on top of that. Fetal heartbeats during labor are usually about 140 per minute. They may speed up at times but slowing down is much more ominous and is an indication of fetal suffering. We listened for "dips" in the heart rates during labor to determine if our patient would need to be sent to more specialized care or a caesarian in *Queretaro City*.

Women who came in for delivery but also wanted a post-partum tubal ligation would also be sent to *Queretaro City*. Even though Mexico is a Catholic country and theoretically against birth control, the Mexican government was, I believe, ahead of its times and encouraged mothers who already had five or six babies to have a postpartum tubal ligation, leaving only a tiny "band aid" scar. The husband's approval was not needed for this surgery.

Old-fashioned Mexican husbands sometimes acted as if their masculinity was threatened if their wives stopped giving birth and tended to be against any form of birth control.

One woman told me, after her post-partum tubal ligation, "I just told him that was the incision from the caesarian!" Asked if her husband had really believed the baby's head had fit through that tiny incision, she said he wasn't very bright about female matters.

One day after working at the clinic/hospital for four months or so, two pregnant women came in around the same time, both in labor. That was not very unusual. I had handled two births at the same time before. This time, one of them, Senora Flores, checked out fine. Although she was only a couple inches dilated she would be sent by ambulance to Queretaro Hospital because she wanted a post-partum tubal ligation. When I examined Senora Vasquez's vagina I got a big surprise! I felt two little feet instead of the head I was expecting!

"This is a special case," I said in Spanish. "This baby is a footling!"

I radioed to *Queretaro City* to get direction and to give them the details of the two women we were transferring to them: Senora Vasquez with the footling pregnancy and Senora Flores for eventual delivery and a post-partum tubal ligation.

The ambulance was readied quickly. I accompanied the women to give medical care en route and took a big packet of gauze and extra gloves. Senora Flores got into the ambulance calmly, but Senora Vasquez was already having contractions every three minutes. We went quickly with the siren blasting, maintaining contact with Queretaro Hospital all the while.

Ten minutes out, Senora Vasquez's baby was progressing; the feet were almost completely out of the vagina, but the rest of the body needed to follow shortly. I encouraged her to push because if the baby's head didn't come out it could lead to its demise. In another fifteen minutes most of the body was out. Then labor seemed to decrease. Apparently with much of the body already through the canal, the stimulus to push had diminished. The little body seemed dark colored and not as pink as I would have preferred. Senora Vasquez needed some help!

With no nurse there, I spoke to Senora Flores in a commanding voice, saying in Spanish, "I want you to take your hands and I want you to push Senora Vasquez's baby out now! Push down hard on her belly right here, now!"

Senora Flores did exactly as ordered without saying a word. Although not normally the best practice, manually helping move the baby along is sometimes done. In this case, the procedure did seem to help the baby come out.

The ambulance still had about ten minutes to go and the baby was finally born! But to my dismay, it wasn't crying and it wasn't pink. I had never performed mouth-to-mouth resuscitation on a baby before but I had trained for it. I had already used up all the gauze, but I grabbed that little blue baby covered with afterbirth, and I put my lips around his mouth and nose and blew in repeatedly and rhythmically. He seemed to react favorably.

Rounding the last bend into Queretaro Hospital, the baby was now pink and starting to cry. I must have looked like a monster with blood all over my lips and face! But hospital nurses and doctors came out to welcome us and cheered and clapped! We were heroes!

Senora Vasquez and her baby were alive and well. Senora Flores was fine too, and I was told she is normally a very talkative person. I must have scared the poor woman into silence, but I gave her an experience she could talk about for the rest of her life.

## NO MORE CATSUP PLEASE

At one time in my medical career, I was a part-time coroner. The pay was not great, but the county would reimburse expenses for continuing education, so every so often I would go away to a conference specific to my vocation.

On one particularly memorable time the theme of the conference was profiling, a new concept at the time. The venue was in Allentown, Pennsylvania. I entered the hotel conference room in a bright, shiny mood eager to learn more about my new occupation. As a doctor, I have long been used to dealing with death and the dying, and such things don't usually affect me much. It's simply part of my job. But this time was different.

Standing in front of us at the podium, the speaker calmly and methodically described every detail of the grisly murder of an entire family, a crime so terrible it could only have been done by a psychopath. No one in their right mind could have imagined doing what this person did, yet at first, authorities had no idea where to look. The speaker described how the use of profiling techniques helped to find such culprits.

He went on to tell how, when investigators went into the house where the crimes took place, they found a gory scene with both husband and wife hacked to death as well as their baby. The murderer had cut up the bodies and washed the pieces off in the bathtub. The big clue here was the tub, which had a bloody ring around it showing it had been wiped off in a fashion similar to how mental hospitals teach their patients to clean up after themselves.

Using this and other information, the profiler was able to determine that the murderer had recently been discharged from a mental hospital and could be found within a two to three mile radius. Indeed, all he had said turned out to be true and the culprit was quickly apprehended.

The whole case was horrifying, and I worked hard to keep my composure and not let fellow coroners know I was distressed. What I found especially disconcerting was that the baby's body parts had been placed in a fast-food fried chicken container, and there was a catsup bottle in the kitchen full of the victims' blood!

I couldn't help thinking of my own two children, and how lucky I was they'd made it safely this far, unlike the poor baby in this case, and with crazy psychopaths roaming the streets freely. Being a mother, this was more than I could comfortably deal with. It was getting late and I just wanted to go home. As soon as the speaker started winding down, I hurried to get out of there as quickly as possible.

It only takes an hour and a half to drive from Allentown to Bloomsburg, Pennsylvania, but I was getting quite tired. Surprisingly, in spite of all the horrific details of the case presented, I was also getting very hungry. There was a brightly lit Wendy's fast food restaurant nearby, so I pulled over and went inside. Nothing seemed amiss at first so I ordered a Pepsi, to keep me more alert for the trip.

After traumatic events, there's something comforting about revisiting places you're used to, and this was the same as all the other Wendy's I'd been to before. The leather seat was soft and warm; the employees had their same brightly colored outfits; and the customers were happily munching on hamburgers and fries.

Suddenly I was dragged out of my transient moment of calm by a horrifying sight: **there was a bottle of catsup on every table!**

I should have foreseen it, but I was not ready to subject myself to the thoughts catsup would bring flooding back. I closed my eyes for a few minutes, but finally reopened them and called the waitress over.

"She'll think I'm totally bonkers!" I thought, but after a brief explanation I asked her to remove all catsup bottles from my view. She complied, and only then was I able to eat my meal and get on my way.

Slowly, ever so slowly, over the months and years since, catsup bottles have lost their sinister look and have returned to normalcy. Once I began eating catsup again, I knew the healing was complete.

# DOREEN KENNEDY

A recent transplant to the Antelope Valley from Atlanta, Georgia, Doreen currently spends her time juggling educational volunteer work with her passion for writing short stories. She majored in Math and Physics as a teen, and after a twenty-five year career as a technical writer, decided it was time for a change. She returned to college, Kennesaw State University in Georgia, and received her degree in English, Secondary Education, with a minor in Professional Writing.

Doreen has always loved to read and has written since she could first hold a pencil. She has written every kind of document for every kind of industry – computers, communications, optics, lottery games, financial, industrial, marketing, educational, and contractors for the U.S. Air Force, Army, Navy, and NASA. Her documentation has received numerous awards and accolades.

Doreen enjoys all genres of writing, but particularly favors humor and satire. Among her many writing projects, she is working on publishing a collection of short stories based on the experiences of women.

## ANT IN A CUP

One glorious morning I sat to enjoy one of life's great and still legal pleasures: coffee. It was the real thing. Dark, rich, caffeinated sin in a cup. Pure roasted, fresh ground beans. Not manipulated into decaf or half-caf, no formaldehyde residue, no synthesized syrups. A True Brew!

As my thumb stroked the smooth comforting warmth, something tickled my forefinger. I pulled back. A large ant was jogging around the rim of my favorite mug. The nerve! I shall spoil that bug's fun like it just ruined my morning pick-me-up. But wait a second, if I swat it I could spill my precious brew, or even worse - break my favorite mug. What a dilemma.

But before I could consider my options, that ant climbed upon the lip of my cup, stopped and stared straight at me. Just stared with its bug eyes while its sticky ant feet left bug footprints where my coffee-craving lips should have been. Then, without any warning, it dived - straight into my steaming brew! I watched as its tiny appendages twitched in a sort of panic stricken back stroke, and soon the lifeless bug body just floated - swirling slowly in a whirlpool of ruined Italian blend.

The end came quickly. Yet I continued to gaze at it like some rubber-necking motorist at an accident scene. Any normal person would have just tossed it out and got another cup, but I am not normal. I fixated upon this creature and its untimely death in my coffee mug. Was it a scout sent to find bounty in my kitchen and report back to the hill to plan an all-out attack? Fooled you, bug! Not much to write home about in my kitchen. Maybe it couldn't handle the disappointment. Maybe it was premeditated. The lowly scout could not return to face the disgrace and humiliation of the queen ant and decided to end it all.

I wonder what killed it so quickly? The heat? The oily surface? Or perhaps the massive shock of caffeine to its tiny nervous system. How sad, I could have saved that ant. A more alert mind would have noticed its intentions, keener eyesight would have seen those six feet teetering on the brink of disaster ..., but alas, I did not have my morning coffee.

## THE DOG'S CHAIR

"That's the dog's chair," says my date for the evening.

"He must be joking." I say to myself.

"You can't sit there. That's the dog's chair," he repeats, poking his head out the kitchen doorway. "Mind sitting over there?" He points to a worn futon, the only other seat in his scantily furnished apartment.

My immediate answer should have been, "Yes I mind," and my next move out the door. Instead I shoot him a raised eyebrow that he doesn't even notice. He is too busy scratching the head of Merlin, his mixed Labrador, who must have trotted into the kitchen to squeal on me. The dog leaps onto the soft leather, oversized armchair to enjoy the nice warm seat I'd left for him. Meanwhile I move to the hard uncomfortable futon opposite what I swear is Merlin's gloating grin.

'That-a-boy, Mer," he says in his *best-buddy* voice as he pats the big dog roughly on the back – the way guys do to each other when they're playing football, or baseball, or some kind of ball where they swat each other on the butt and then all go out for beers.

My date heads back into the kitchen, hopefully to get my forgotten drink. I sure do need it. Maybe he's just going to get a beer for Merlin. And here I am - drinkless and alone on this log disguised as a sofa. Hopefully he's too preoccupied to notice that, behind my blank stare, my thought processes are plotting an early escape.

Oops, too late. He plops next to me on the log, like some playful bear cub, nearly dousing me with his Coors. As his arm creeps around my back to pull me closer, I am watching Merlin watching us with green jealous doggie eyes. Someone help me. I need some kind of a distraction. If I can only get Merlin out of that chair!

"I believe you forgot my drink," I politely inform my neglectful host.

"So sorry. What was I getting you?"

"Wine cooler, please."

"Oh, yeah." And as he struts back to the kitchen singing offkey to the Beach Boys *In my Room*, I put my plan into action. Merlin's eyes had followed him as he walked to the kitchen, and I could only hope that the dog wanted a snack more than just his owner's attention. Thank goodness I still have that half-pack of LifeSavers in the bottom of my purse. They are old, stale, and covered with crumbs, fuzz balls, and goodness knows what kind of grit that lurks in the bottom of a woman's handbag. I hold out the first lint encrusted disk with my fingers.

"Here boy, here Mer, come get it," I whisper, my hand extended toward the animal now sitting up in what should be my comfy chair. Merlin looks, but doesn't budge.

"*Hurry up and get out of the damn chair, dog*," I was about to say when a voice once again yells from the kitchen, "Sorry, no wine coolers. But I can open a bottle of wine."

"Sure. Got red?"

"Nope. Only buy white. Red stains the carpet."

Probably feeds the wine to the dog, too. I can't believe he lets this horse of a dog on his furniture, yet he worries about his carpet. That's it! The carpet.

"Here, Mer, go fetch." And I toss the candy as far as I can throw it, which isn't too far since it sticks to my fingers. But it finally releases and takes a good bounce off the end table. The heavy coating of purse lint keeps it from breaking. Better yet, Merlin takes the bait. As he leaps for the treat, I hop into his comfy chair, just as my glass of stain proof wine finally appears.

"Hey, you moved. And what's Merlin eating. Here boy, here, bring it to daddy."

Daddy? As much as I need that drink, it is definitely time to check out. "I hate to do this to you, but I think something I ate earlier isn't agreeing with my stomach, and…"

"It's a nasty piece of candy! Where'd you get this Mer?" He hasn't heard a word I said.

"I gave it to him," I proudly declare. "I was about to have a Lifesaver and he looked at me like he wanted one, too. So I..."

"So you gave my dog candy? Do you know what that can do to his system? I'll have to sit up all night and watch him now, damn it!"

I quickly stood from what was now a big comfy lesson in the dating game. "Like I said, I have to leave now."

"Well there's the door, don't let it hit ya..."

Oh! It was soooo a snappy comeback moment. But he wouldn't have heard me anyway. He was sitting in the dog's chair with Merlin draped across his lap as he massaged the creature's over sensitive tummy.

Lesson learned: next date, first question: Do you have a dog?

## INDEPENDENCE DAY

Strange, how one of the worst days of your life can turn out to be one of the best days.

On this particular day, a certain office store was having a "come and spend your money on worthless junk that we usually throw away" sale - otherwise known as a Sidewalk Sale. Typically I would be on the buying end of such events, but today I was the seller - a lowly minimum wage employee of said office store after being laid off from a once great-paying technical job. Things were bad enough. I went from meetings in the board room to scrubbing the store bathrooms. The only good part of that chore was being able to hide from everyone in the restrooms.

But today my degradation was complete. I was outside, in full view of the world, spending my work day with the Oscar Mayer Weinermobile. Yes, there I stood, in my store logo shirt that made me look like a 1960's gas station attendant, passing out sales flyers in front of the famous wiener on wheels.

Wait, it gets worse. The two "Hot Doggers," that's what they call the crazy kids who get paid to tour with the Big Dog, leaned out the "bun roof" every so often and tossed "wiener whistles" to the waiting arms below.

And---it gets even worse. Before those eager sidewalk shoppers could rush home with their treasured souvenir whistles, I had to make them sing, "Oh I wish I were..." DEAD! Right there. Right then. Just cover me in ketchup and kick my body under the big bun's wheels before my own two kids see me.

But here comes the silver lining in my wiener cloud. Today made me realize that: (1) I don't ever want to drive around in or ever be seen with a vehicle shaped like meat, (2) I no longer want to sell stuff that I hate, or make other people buy stuff that we both hate, and (3) I don't want to spend the rest of my life working for someone else, especially if it means standing in front of a giant wiener.

So I went home that evening and applied to go back to college, and then I went to said office store the next day and put in my notice. A great ending to an awful day.

## DIETING

Had I been thinking at all, I would be seated on the other side of the restaurant in the section behind the plastic-ivy—away from prying eyes, happily devouring my chicken strip special. Instead, a mere empty table separates us.

The other diners ignore him, like the young couple with the toddler climbing over a booth with a mouthful of french fries, or the couple munching like oversized gerbils on a 10-piece box of fried chicken. They all got the message about the strange man in the middle and moved to the dining area's perimeter booths.

Dining area? That deserves an 'lol' for sure. Calling the Quik-Chik a restaurant is like calling the Pinto a classic car. As soon as you enter you gain three pounds just from inhaling the grease-laden air. The eat-in area is a scattering of tables in the center with booths lining the walls. A kiddie play area, probably used for birthday parties, is semi-private due to a plastic-plant partition. No party today. Why didn't I sit there? Why did I come in here in the first place? Because they make the best darn fried chicken – thick and crunchy on the outside, juicy and meaty on the inside. A dieter's wet dream! And in a moment of weakness I slipped into the Quik-Chik with every intention of cheating on my doctor-prescribed meal plan – only I was too preoccupied with who might see me, to see him.

He is thin and unshaven, obviously a drifter. A thick, untrimmed beard covers the sunken areas of his face making it difficult to figure his age - 20s? 30s? Maybe 40s? Long hair pulled into a ponytail hangs over his brown t-shirt which is creased as if it were pulled out of a laundry hamper or from under a bed. Just as crumpled are his gray sweat pants. They are torn and frayed at the cuffs where they hang over his well-used athletic shoes, the kind I throw away when my hubby buys new ones. But the biggest giveaway to his social status – he is talking to himself. Not loudly, but carrying on a normal conversation with the three empty chairs around his table. I've read that some homeless people have a mental illness, and I'm not sure what I feel more – sorrow or fear.

I keep my head down, forcing me to examine my 1500 calorie lunch. I am awash in grease and guilt. As I eat, I watch that drifter from the corner of my eye. His table is clean, but he does have a drink, a small paper cup, not the super-sized ones that most men order. He takes short, slow sips, probably to make it last longer. I notice a gym bag on the chair next to him. I bet that's where he keeps the rest of his wrinkled wardrobe and probably his few possessions.

Suddenly he sets the drink down, props his head in his hands, and stares directly at me. Has he caught me staring, or are his hollow eyes fixed on my paper plate full of fried chicken strips, onion rings, and a side of slaw? Way too much food for my body to consume; no doubt more food than he's had in a week. I quickly turn away and re-examine my previous cravings for grease and salt. Sure I was getting tired of plain yogurt, but with fresh berries and a little honey it's not so bad. It's also not too late. Have I the nerve to give this poor man my leftovers? They're untouched. Will he be appreciative or angered?

I raise my right eyebrow to check on the homeless man – he's gone. I look up and all around and spot him outside leaning against one of the windows. And he is smoking! Well, I thought, he's near starving but he has money to buy cigarettes. Here I was feeling sorry for this guy. But maybe someone gave him a cigarette. He's coming back inside. His drink is still on the table. Of course, that drink must be his ticket to sit there as long as he can.

I realize I have eaten only one chicken strip. I should pay this guy to follow me around all day. He'd have a job, money in his pocket, free food, and in return I will be so guilt-ridden that I stay on my diet. I'm actually not hungry anymore. That settles it. I'm going to give him my food. Not just to be charitable to a homeless person, but to thank him for keeping me on the straight and narrow.

I pack up my chicken and sides and proudly congratulate myself for what I am about to do. Food in hand, I walk towards his table just as a young man barges through the door and blocks my route. He heads straight for the drifter.

"Hey Ed, hope you ain't been waitin' long? "Grab your bag and let's go; the other team's probably already there."

Then he and my 'drifter' rush out to a waiting SUV full of more young men, one of them tossing a football in the front seat.

I dump the chicken strips, with the onion rings and the coleslaw, into the nearest trash can along with all of my assumptions.

# OLEG KAGAN

Oleg Kagan is a writer, librarian, and web designer. His prose and poetry have appeared in several anthologies including *Rokoko*, *Saturation*, *Ohmanut*, *Westwind*, *Phantom Seeds,* and his Haiku in others, including the Southern California Haiku Study Group yearly anthologies and occasional keepsakes.

Oleg, now a librarian with the West Hollywood branch of the County of Los Angeles Library System, is proud to be the founder of the Lancaster Library Writers Group (now known as the Antelope Valley Writers Association). Originally from Kyiv, Ukraine, he lives with his wife Ashley in the Mar Vista neighborhood of Los Angeles, California.

## AT THE MUSEUM STORE, SHE

At the museum store, she
lifts the paperweight
and puts it down inches
from its previous place.


She thinks about the art
at the museum store. She
remembers how it felt,
when she first saw that weight.


Having spent so much time
examining objects
at the museum store, she
wakes into a dream where


there are many of her
milling around a room
for an exhibit called
"At the museum: She."

OLEG'S HAIKU:
(One for each season)


fog layer
the barista pulls me
another shot


shouting down
each other's shouts --
hail storm


planting time --
the tattooed man
discovers a place


lazy afternoon
before the punchline
trailing off...

MY FIRST ASSIGNMENT

When I found out that my first assignment as a professional librarian was going to be at the Lancaster Library, I went home and searched Google Maps for the city. When it came into view, I had to zoom out several times to see both it and my neighborhood on the same map. I groaned at its distance from North Hollywood, where I was living.

Driving up Route 14 and into the Antelope Valley for the first time, I almost lost a hand when I opened my window and stuck a few fingers out into the wind. Apparently, I should have taken the howling gusts as a warning. That drive was also the first time I ever saw a tumbleweed outside of a cartoon. "They really exist," I shouted to my friends when I got back. I saw train tracks, big empty blocks, and the Thai Cafe, as I drove up Sierra Highway before making a left onto Lancaster Blvd. This was well before it became THE BLVD with trendy shops and restaurants and cars parked down the middle.

I was on Lancaster Blvd, and there it was, near the middle of the strip between Sierra Hwy and 10th Street, the Library. Unassuming on the outside, but inside a dream if judged by size, (Lancaster still boasts the largest library building in the County of Los Angeles Library System). I was given a tour, introduced to the staff, and *poof!*, I was back in the car driving the sixty miles back to Los Angeles. I thought about how other librarians told me that working in Lancaster was...interesting. "And it's way up there," they would say. I listened and was nonplussed. I'd been shelving books at a library in the middle of Hollywood for almost ten years. I'd seen everything. In truth, I was excited!

As it turned out, spending almost two years working in the Antelope Valley was a wonderful first assignment. True, it was close to reality when I told people back then that I practically lived in my car -- not, mind you, by way of complaint. I was always driving against the traffic into a big beautiful sky, and I was able to listen to more audio books than ever. It was a pleasure for me, but not for my car, which suffered a heart attack at 127,000 miles and had to get a time-consuming and costly transplant before once more braving the commute. But more important than anything, my destination was a fulfilling job.

A large part of that fulfillment came from a small writers group I founded in the library's Literacy Room. Part of my motivation was selfish; the commute had edged out my previous writing group, and I required the company of writers. Equally decisive was a hunch that there had to be plenty of scribblers and would-be scribblers in the Valley that had no place to go. Community is important for creative people, and though I knew there were other writers groups in the area, I sensed that there was still a need.

Naturally, I had no idea when I made the first PA announcement, that such a terrific group would be born. Not only was listening to everyone's work frequently the highlight of my week, but seeing friendships form -- bonds that went beyond writing -- is what makes me so proud to have started the Antelope Valley Writers group.

And now that I have read *Soaring*, their first anthology, I feel privileged to have experienced something few librarians get to experience. So often when we are given a new assignment, the work we did at our previous library disappears. The old library is in the past, and it is not in the nature of the profession to expect anything else. Buildings, after all, have no memory. And yet, here I am closing the anthology of the Antelope Valley Writers Association (their new name). It's the result of dedicated people harnessing their creative powers to author, compile, edit, and publish a book. Is there a better gift for a librarian? I don't think so. Thank you.

*THE END*

# INDIVIDUAL COPYRIGHTS